INFINITE LOVE

Front cover picture courtesy of http://www.pdphoto.org

Copyright © 2008 All That Is - Angela Thorne
All rights reserved.
ISBN: 1-4196-5120-X
ISBN-13: 978-1419651205

ANGELA THORNE

INFINITE LOVE
BOOK II
DIVINE MESSAGES FROM
ALL THAT IS

2008

INFINITE LOVE

TABLE OF CONTENTS

I Dedicate This Book To The

Oneness Of Love That We All Are

And To The Memory Of The

Only One Self

That Exists.

PREFACE

Numerous messages have been received from ALL THAT IS over the past few years. Most were received during gatherings, workshops and seminars but a few were directly dictated.

I was told that the teachings received were to be shared through a Trilogy of Books as a reminder of the Trinity of Self that we are on Earth. First, there must be Wisdom, or Inspiration, for without Inspiration or Wisdom enlightened choices can not be made. Second, there must be a Remembrance of the nature of Love in order for us to recognize our True Selves or our Divine nature. And third, there must be Action to bring about Fulfillment of any chosen path or goal. If any of these is incomplete, the outcome will be incomplete. The messages contained in this book fall into the second category and are, therefore, gifts to remind us of our true nature.

The words contained in all of these messages have been vibrationally charged and will assist all who are ready to know a grander truth. Only very minor editing has been done to this material since I was asked to share the messages in the manner they were given. The use of capital letters and highlighted words are for emphasis and importance, as was recommended while being transcribed. Some dates, as well as questions, were not recorded and consequently can not be shown, while some of the questions have been condensed for easier reading.

My sincere thanks to all, on all planes of existence, who participated in allowing this information to be made available and for bringing awareness of it to those who may be ready to return to the Divine. We have collectively asked for help, therefore collectively, we are the authors of this information. May we continue to spread our Love throughout the Universe so that Peace may reign supreme.

I offer this book to ALL in Love, Praise, and Thanksgiving for all that we are and all that we can ever BE. May we walk together in harmony always and all ways. And So It Shall Be Done.

I Am All That Is Angela.

INTRODUCTION

*I*nfinite Wisdom, Book I of our series, consisted of messages and techniques to assist in creating changes, if one so chooses. *Infinite Love,* Book II, is a reminder to all that we have come from Love and that we must return to Love. These are messages that you have heard before but are now being presented in a more expanded way to allow your consciousness to also expand and, therefore, remember what has simply been forgotten.

LOVE is the only TRUE ENERGY existing in the Universe. Every thing that exists MUST therefore be an aspect of this energy which is called Love, and the only reason for establishing names for things is for identification purposes. Names have been created to bring awareness to the varying aspects of Love and for no other reason. Names are to distinguish the differences of this one true Energy.

Because LOVE is ENERGY in its purest form, it is often believed that the somewhat less pure states, or aspects, are not Love. But energy is never constant to the observer because the observer is also the very energy that is never constant. When, however, the observer and the observed are in harmony, one with the other, an energetic state arises which man has labeled as Love, when in reality it is simply the meeting of two harmoniously vibrating aspects of the only existing energy, as opposed to aspects that are not vibrationally conducive.

Humanity, during its earthly existence, has chosen to give names to these varying vibrations of the only true energy in order to identify these numerous combinations. In reality, every thing is simply LOVE in numerous combinations. When humanity ceases to separate through distinction, humanity will return to the awareness of the Oneness of all things in spite of the varying colors and hues and shapes and sizes and dimensions that presently exist on this plane of awareness.

This **Oneness** is the Truth of Infinite Love. You are being reminded of the Truth of your existence, of the Truth of your reality, of the Truth of WHO you are. By acknowledging, and embracing, and living this Truth, you allow YOU to return to LOVE.

But I have given you Free Will to choose to return to LOVE or choose not to return to LOVE. It is your choice.

And It Is So. And It Is So. And It Is So.

For I Am ALL THAT IS, And I Say So.

CHAPTER 1
IMAGE AND LIKENESS

Once again, My thanks to you for being here to share in the Word and to share with others your word.

You were created in the IMAGE and LIKENESS
Of God Almighty,
Mother/Father Creator,
ALL THAT IS.

What a difficult theory for My Spirit Beings to accept.
Not only can they not accept that each is a *symbol*
Born out of the Image and Likeness of God,
But that every thing around
Is born out of the
Image and Likeness of God.

That is why I am asking to be referred to as
ALL THAT IS
So that My Spirit Beings may begin
To grasp the enormity of Who they are,
And of Who I AM.

Anything that exists in the Universe is existing because of the energy created by God. And if everything is energy, and everything is created by energy, it stands to reason that We are each representing an Image and a Likeness of God. You have all been created EQUAL, each as energy. But energy in the form of matter must distinguish itself in various ways and there are many various *images and likenesses* in the form of matter that exist on your planet Earth.

What man is seeking to do with the energy that is called matter differentiates positive from negative. Just as one man's garbage is another man's GOLD, so too, what one may see as unworthy, another may find beneficial. What one may consider ugly, another may observe the beauty within. What one may call disastrous, another will acknowledge as a gift—for beauty lies within.

Beauty can only be seen through the eyes of beauty. Non-beauty will be seen by those who have not yet discovered BEAUTY. Does it make what one calls beauty any more beautiful or any less beautiful than that which is observed by the other? Everything is an aspect and created equal in the eyes of God. Your earthly experience causes you to recognize what ever you are able to recognize. Seek to observe through the eyes of Beauty and there will be great beauty to behold.

That will be My lesson to you tonight. May your eyes BEHOLD the BEAUTY that lies within. May your eyes behold the Beauty in the Image and Likeness of God. May your eyes see the Glory of God.

And It Is So. And It Is So. And It Is So.

March 6, 1999

CHAPTER 2
ATTACHED TO EARTHLY THINKING

I thank you once again for taking the time to want to share in this experience. How attached we are to our conditioned way of thinking! How difficult it is for My Spirit Beings to embrace a change in their mode of thinking! What a strong pull this earthly realm holds for My Spirit Beings!

Is it fear of the unknown that causes one not to seek to make changes? Or is it the fear of not being a part of the society that we call "friends"? We become so attached to the earthly way of thinking that we cannot bear to pull ourselves away.

This is going to be a very short message today. I would like you to think about the reasons why as Spirit Beings there is such a pull to this earthly existence, away from your true home, away from your true existence. Why is it so difficult when you are here visiting this spirit realm that the very thought of non-attachment to anything that you have grown accustomed to causes such conflict? Why is it that it becomes so very difficult to even pay attention to the words of wisdom that are shared with you by the many teachers? Why is it so very difficult? And what can be done about it? And I will leave you to ponder those thoughts this week.

May your days ahead be filled with Peace and Love and Joy. May you come to know Peace and Love and Joy and exist in Light and Love.

And It Is So. And It Is So. And It Is So.

March 13, 1999

CHAPTER 3
YOU ARE IN THIS REALM BY CHOICE

I thank you so very much for being here to share your Divine energy with others. It is so powerful when groups can get together to share healing with each other. It is even more powerful when groups can get together and share healing from the heart rather than through obligation, and I know that each of you is here tonight to share and to get to know more about the Truth.

The truth is that your existence in this spiritual realm that you call the Earthly realm is to allow you to advance your spiritual nature. You are first and foremost a Spirit Being. You are having a human experience because you know your self to be human while you exist in this earthly plane, but this earthly plane is much more than just an earthly plane, and that is what I would like to emphasize in the next little while.

My Spirit Beings believe that the earthly plane is not a spiritual realm, but the earthly plane must be a spiritual realm for My Spirit Beings to exist in this realm. I would like My Spirit Beings to think of this earthly realm as a spiritual realm rather than just an earthly realm. By doing so it may bring them into greater focus of WHO they really are. There are many, many opportunities here in this earthly realm to allow you to perfect your virtues. For those who are not aware of this process, I have explained in the past that you are here on Earth to perfect virtues. And you have chosen certain virtues to work on and to perfect before you return to your home in the HIGHER spiritual realm.

It is My desire at this time to emphasize that whatever lessons or remembrance or awareness that you come into through this existence must be "Spiritual Awareness." You must go beyond the human way of thinking. Go beyond Jane and John and Jimmy and Mary. **See each other as Spirit Beings helping each other to perfect their virtues.**

You have all come to this realm by choice. Your Soul, to simplify it of course, is seeking to know it Self to be greater than who or what it was, and by being in this spiritual realm called Earth you have the many, many opportunities to get to understand self, to get to see your selves in different ways and to learn from what you see.

I am encouraging you all to see the situations and circumstances that are brought to you as GIFTS to allow you to know greater Spiritual Truths. See each situation and circumstance as an opportunity to get to know more about where you are and where you would like to be, or who you are and who you would like to be-come. See each situation and circumstance as an opportunity to develop greater skills. See each situation and circumstance as an opportunity to strive for greater spiritual awareness.

You are so much more than human. Your greatest gift lies within. That is where you will get to know the grandest truths. In order to be able to understand the truths you must be able to get to the place where you can even know the truth. And how can you get there?...*Through an avenue of healing, through meditation, through praying, through changing your thoughts.*

As I have said in the past, and as I will remind you over and over again, your thoughts are prayers. **Your thoughts are**

prayers. They are the most profound aspect of your self. You use this aspect of self unceasingly. You must, therefore, observe thoughts and change the thoughts that are not serving you at this time to become who you would like to become, and seek to embrace the thoughts that are going to be worthy of your spiritual desires.

Seek to embrace the opportunities that are given to you through the many conflicts of life. Those present the greatest opportunities for growth. See them as spiritual gifts. Seek to understand what they mean. Seek to understand what they are showing you about your selves. And seek to learn, seek to change. By doing so, you will be healing the Universe.

You may ask, *'Why is it necessary for me to heal the Universe?'* And My answer to you would have to be, **"Because you are ONE with the Universe."** You are One with each other and you are One with the Universe. However one thinks, affects the rest of the Universe. However one heals, affects the rest of the Universe. As you thinketh, so shall you be. As you healeth, so shall you be. If each is connected, the thoughts of one will greatly affect the thoughts of the whole. The healing of one will magnify the healing of the whole.

You have within you the capacity to move mountains. You just do not believe that you have within you the capacity to move mountains. You must understand Self. Understand the components of Self; get to understand who you really are and work at developing who you are so that you may experience who you are to the fullest capacity possible. And you may do so in many different ways.

There are as many religions as there are groups of people seeking to understand. There are as many writers as there are groups of people seeking to know the truth. There are as many Masters as there are groups desiring to know the truth. Seek and you shall find. Knock and it will be granted unto you..... Simple, but profound.

I have given My Spirit Beings everything that they need for this journey here into this spiritual realm. I have created Laws to assist. You must seek to use the Laws to your greatest advantage.

And I will pause here to allow you to ask any questions that you may choose to ask.

Question: 'Is healing trying to change another?'

It is important to understand that you cannot change another. What you do with healing, whether it is through healing prayers or physical healing, is bringing more positive or divine energy to that Spirit Being. What you are doing is calling on Divine connections to assist that Spirit Being. You are asking for the energy to be magnified on behalf of the Spirit Being and by doing so, the Spirit Being will have greater opportunities to make changes, but you do not make changes for another. What you are doing as healers is bringing more light, bringing more love, bringing more positive energy into the area of the Spirit Being.

Some of My Spirit Beings consider there to be angels or entities—there are so many interpretations. But there are Divine Beings who assist with healing, and by prayer, it's magnifying the call for help, so to speak, so that greater energy and assistance can be given to that person. Therefore, more energy will flow, even if the person is not aware that they can ask for this themselves. You are assisting them, you are helping them, but you are not changing them. It is up to them if they would like to accept the information or energy that is being given to them. And changes will come to them through understanding. And this is what happens through healing of this nature. You remove the blocked energy and allow greater awareness to flow...awareness that you already have within you.

Awareness does not come from outside of Self. Awareness is already within who you are. You just have not been tapping into it, so by doing healings or participating in healings you are allowing the energy to break up to allow greater awareness to flow in. It's like opening up a tap, so to speak. Or, as your humanity now knows, cleaning out your blood vessels to allow the awareness to flow. But it's everything that you already have.

Some of My Spirit Beings may not even want to pay attention but it is very rare that with extra energy coming to them, with extra information coming to them from a divine source, that they do not make some changes. Some will make bigger changes, and others will make smaller changes, depending on the capacity of the Spirit Being being prayed for, or being healed, to want to be healed. But one can not change another, unless another wants to be changed. And as you continue to grow spiritually, you will realize that each is here for a specific purpose and one is responsible for one's self and not for another's spiritual growth, except in the capacity to allow them to get to know themselves as who they really are.

Question regarding the well-being of someone who passed on suddenly and, therefore, the lack of opportunity for the parents to express what was in their hearts.

Everything is always okay when Spirit Beings no longer inhabit the human form. It is just a transference of energy, so to speak. You are a Spirit; you have assumed a human body for this earthly existence; you no longer want to participate in this earthly existence; you depart this earthly body and go back to your home. So there is no need to be concerned with those who are no longer in the human realm. But because of a lack of understanding on the parts of those who are still here in the human realm they become quite concerned for the welfare and safety of the Spirit Being. But when one understands that one chooses to come to this spiritual land called Earth; one chooses one's family; one chooses the virtues; and, therefore, one also chooses the exit; that there are really no accidents in the Universe. But because of the limiting capacity of man, it is believed that this is the greatest realm, and then as one departs from this realm one is less fortunate. But the truth is, one is at greater peace because one is truly moving towards a greater light as one departs from the darkness of this earthly realm.

In the Spirit realm one is connected through thought, and just as the thoughts of those in the earthly realm would bring the energy of the Spirit Being back to that area, whatever they are thinking about would also project them to that area. So when they are not embodied within this human mass, their thoughts have faster projection. If one thinks about someone and wants to send them a message, by all means go right ahead and send them the message and accept that they will hear it, just as one must accept that when one speaks to one's God, that God is hearing. And Trust is believing that God hears without getting an answer.

Brief discussion about Easter and Jesus.

Easter is again one of those celebrations just like Ash Wednesday—it is purely man-made, purely man-made. And as I spoke on our last meeting I will not elaborate on that aspect again but to remind you that because it is man-made it is based on man's understanding of a particular issue.

Question: 'Will the entity that was called Jesus be returning to Earth?'

Yes, the entity that was known as Jesus will be returning to Earth. Whether you recognize him will be seen at the time! But the entity that was Jesus was also other entities as well.

Question: 'So Jesus had several lives?'

Absolutely, absolutely. Just as you have had thousands of lives, Jesus had several lives. Jesus was in human form. He came with a very profound message on My behalf. He came to show a way of life to My Spirit Beings on Earth, to assist them in knowing the truth, but there were also other Spirit Beings who came to share the truth as well.

Question: 'Any we can recognize?'...'Krishna, Muhammad?'

Any others you think?

Response: 'Gandhi? Mother Teresa? Ram? Mandela?'

Yes, some with greater truths than others, but all sharing an aspect of truth, all sharing an aspect of Truth. All sharing the Word as it was given to them, for them to share with others.

Question: 'Is the present Pope a messenger as well?' (Pope John Paul II at the time of the recording.)

You must accept that all Spirit Beings are messengers. You are a messenger, and you are a messenger. Each and every one of you is a messenger, but sharing different messages; different magnitudes of message, but each a message, each a message.

Comment that some messengers have a wider audience but that messages could also be from someone on stage, or singing.

Yes, but some bring greater Truths. What I am explaining is that as one progresses in this spiritual realm that you call Earth one moves beyond certain truths. There are some of My Spirit Beings who believe that Jesus is God, and that one can not get to God Almighty except through Jesus. That is their truth, as they can understand it; otherwise they will not embrace it. When you can get to the point of questioning, *'Why do I have to go through Jesus to get to God?'* then you know that you are ready to move on to a greater Truth, because Jesus was here as a Messenger to say, "I am One with the Father, and so can you be." You do not have to go through Jesus to get to God Almighty.

Jesus was an entity, as you are an entity. If Jesus can become One with God, you too can become One with God. In fact, you are each One with God, but you have not gotten to the level of understanding for you to accept that you are One with God, God Almighty. For your Soul is also your God within, connecting you to God Almighty. **Your Soul is also your God within connecting you to God Almighty,** in simple terms. And then as a result we are all connected, because we are all part of God. Therefore, what you think about either assists or harms the other because you are all connected through the Divine energy.

Brief discussion regarding the enormity of our connection to each other and to the Universe.

I would like to take this opportunity to thank you for being here and for sharing with others. We will continue to discuss the ways that we may observe the gifts that are being brought to us through situations and circumstances. How we can understand the messages that are being shared with us through our various messengers and how we may use those messages to assist us. It is always quite different when one says that they are gifts to you, but how can you learn from the gifts if you do not understand how to decipher the gifts? We will continue along those lines at another meeting.

May your days ahead be filled with Peace and Love and Light. May Love and Light flow through you. May Love and Light surround you, and may you know your Selves to be One with all of the Light. May your days ahead be filled with the Peace that you seek to know.

And It Is So. And It Is So. And It Is So.

March 17, 1999

CHAPTER 4
FORGETFULNESS

I thank you for being here to share in the Word once again. Last week we spoke about the forgetfulness that is assumed for this journey here on Earth, and through this veil of forgetfulness My Spirit Beings become quite attached to their earthly existence.

I have also shared very briefly that this earthly experience is a spiritual experience. This earthly realm, as you choose to call it, is also a spiritual realm, for the experiences here bring you into greater spiritual growth, and greater spiritual understanding of your Self, or of your Selves

If one can remember what it is truly like where you have come from, you will not be encountering the many difficulties that you face during this journey. Your veil of forgetfulness is truly a very strong and thick veil, but it can be penetrated. Not that you will remember everything about your original existence but you can remember enough to allow you to exist in peace; you can remember enough to allow you to separate Truth from illusion; you can remember enough to have more trust, have more faith, have more understanding. If you can only remember a little of your true existence you will begin to accept each other as parts of your selves, and whatever bothers you about another is what bothers you about self.

We are together on this journey to assist each other in growing, to assist each other in growing. What is your response to whatever your situation or circumstance may indicate to you, is a message to you from the higher aspects of Self. It is a way that the higher aspects of your Being can tell you a little about your self so that you may recognize and make some choices. And those choices will help you to make changes, and those changes will bring you into greater peace and awareness of self.

It is very difficult to be attempting to assist My Spirit Beings and yet not be able to assist My Spirit Beings.

I have shared with you on so many occasions that I will not force My Will on My Spirit Beings but they only have to say the word. They only have to ask; they only have to acknowledge that they are unable to do it on their own and, therefore, need the assistance of the more Divine connection, and assistance will be given. But for those who believe that they have the power solely to accomplish all their goals or to be able to deal with the situations and circumstances that you are facing on a regular basis, without the assistance of the more advanced aspects of who you are, is really living the illusion. For the truth is that you are absolutely nothing without your Divine connection.

That is the Truth whether you would like to accept it or not accept it; whether you would like to believe it and embrace it and live through the truth of that statement, or you would like to deny it and believe that you, who you think you are, really is the all powerful. For those who are able to remember just instinctively, through their spiritual connection, what is the Truth, to those peace will be given, for they instinctively know that they are connected, that they are just an experience here, that they can not do it on their own, but with the greater connection, or with connection to the more Divine through Trust and Faith will begin to see and experience the joy they never knew existed.

I have shared with My Spirit Beings in many different ways that one must ask. One must ASK. But of course, if you believe that you can do it yourself you do not ask, and if you do not ask you do not receive, because the Laws of the Universe have been established for everyone. In all that you do, **ask and you shall receive**.

And that is My lesson to you tonight. I thank you once again for sharing this time with others and I would like to remind you that you are a Spirit Being having a human experience. You have chosen this experience. When the higher aspects of your Being decide that you have completed this experience here on Earth, this experience will be aborted. I must remind you that becoming attached to this earthly experience will only bring you pain. Freedom from attachment to this earthly experience will only bring you Peace and Joy.

LOVE IS ETERNAL. The love you share here on this Earth will be remembered for ever. The lack of love that you share on this Earth will be felt until such time that you can experience more love. The key then is to SHARE LOVE. Share love, for love remains for ever. And that completes My lesson to you tonight unless, of course, you have questions to ask. I take it there are no questions so I will end this session.

And It Is So. And It Is So. And It Is So.

March 27, 1999

CHAPTER 5
STRIVE FOR INTERNAL LIGHT

I thank you very much indeed for taking the time to be here to share your prayers with others and to hear the Word. I have shared with you over the last few years many teachings. I have shown you that you are both positive and negative. I have explained to you that you are electro-magnetic energy. I have explained to you that you are a Spirit Being having a human experience.

I have shared with you the Laws of the Universe and I have given several messages as to how the universe, or how your higher aspects of selves communicate with you to assist you on your journey. This has all been taught to you in the past. You have, however, been given a clearer understanding of the grander truth. Your religions are doing the best that they know. They are sharing the truth as they know and understand.

You have within you the Grandest Truth and you only have to take the time to connect to the Spirit part of you to get whatever answers or whatever direction that you are seeking to know. Some of My Spirit Beings call this the "gut feeling," some call it "intuition," some call it "connecting with the angels," some call it "connecting with your God-mind," some call it "the God-head."

There are as many different names as there are religions. You may call it by any name, as you may choose to call Me by any name, but you will come to realize, at some point, that there is one Creator called by different names, and there is one internal Spirit called by different names. You do not have to accept anyone else's truth, unless you choose to. You only have to go within to know the Grandest Truth.

When you seek to be attached to the more earthly or external situations or circumstances, you are removing your self from connecting with the internal situations or circumstances. As you become intrigued by the external or the more earthly, you take away from the inner connection. In other words, you lose ground. Not that you can ever not be part of your inner connection, but you lose consciousness of your inner connection. The more involved you become with the external, the farther away (*less involved*) you become with the internal.

It is a simple way of understanding this if one would go back to the Earth and the Sun and the Moon. As the revolving takes place, one is either in the light of the Sun or in the light of the Moon. When you are in the light of the Sun, you are outside of the light of the Moon. As you revolve on this planet called Earth, you cannot have both Sun and Moon reflecting their light on you.

The same applies to your consciousness or your awareness of your internal connection and your external stimulation. When one is drawn to the external stimulation, one is withdrawn from the internal; therefore, you lose sense of your awareness of your internal connection. The more you withdraw from the internal, the more of the external that you see, that you become aware of, that you can view, the less aware you become of the internal. The more you strive to be within the Light of the internal, the less you are attracted to the light of the external.

As you have shared a while ago (*through saying a prayer*): "You are the Lamb of God." You are the Eternal Light. You are the Interior Light. You are the Inner Energy, the Inner Flame.

You can choose to gaze inwards and see that Flame or you may choose to look outside. You have been given FREE CHOICE. And that is My lesson to you tonight. And It Is So. And It Is So. And It Is So.

I thank you once again for sharing your love with others. May your days ahead be filled with Peace and Light and Love and may you come to share in the Love that you share with others. For whatever you give away shall be returned to you, tenfold. And It Is So. And It Is So. And It Is So.

Question: 'Why is this ethnic cleansing going on in Yugoslavia?'
(1999)

It has been going on for a very long time and it is a demonstration of the separation that you, as a humanity, believe in. It is simply an expression of what humanity currently believes. When humanity no longer believes in separation; when humanity no longer believes that one race is better or more superior than another, you will no longer need to have these examples brought to you to show you what humanity is believing. For we are all messengers and every thing that exists in the Universe is created by thoughts.

And how will you be shown what your thoughts are except through examples of your thoughts. It works on a personal level, it works on a global level, and it works on a universal level. Everything that is existing around you is an example to you of what is being thought around you, for thoughts are creators, and beliefs are thoughts. Humanity believes in separation; humanity believes in racial dis-harmony; therefore, you must be shown what humanity is currently believing in. Every thing is a message. Every thing is a message.

Question: 'Is Easter also a man-made event, or is it true that Christ died on Good Friday and three days later ascended to heaven?'

The events that took place have not been correctly recorded. Your Easter celebration is based on man's understanding of what took place at that time. When all of this was taking place there was no such thing as Easter. That is why I have explained in the past that Easter is purely man-made, and it is based on man's belief and man's understanding of what occurred at that period in the life of the Spirit Being called Jesus.

(Further questions regarding this issue pursued.)

One must understand the nature of the way things were to fully grasp the truth of what transpired at that time, and I would really encourage you to do some further investigation and get to the truth through another source. All of this occurred a very long, long time ago and just as it is very easy for stories or myths to be told, it is very easy for facts to be changed to suit the story-teller. But there is information available to substantiate the truth surrounding the...

Question/Statement:...'The Passover Plot?'

Yes. One may not get to the truth through books on Christianity, because Christianity is dealing with the crucifixion and resurrection of Christ. They are using that as the basis for their religious beliefs. In order to seek the truth one will have to go outside of the Christian doctrines to have more knowledge of what transpired at the time and to know more about the life of the man called Jesus.

Question (condensed): 'Hypothetically, if the crucifixion of Jesus Christ is symbolic of the relinquishment of attachments or the Soul's desire to free itself from the attachments to the flesh, then is it symbolic, as Carl Jung had propounded, of the pain and suffering that man must endure to know ascension?'

And the answer is symbolically, yes. One must know pain and suffering and one must relinquish earthly attachments in order to be risen again, symbolically.

Some of your churches believe that Christ carried the cross, so therefore, the life that you live is built on carrying crosses until you can become a part of that cross. That is not how it is taught, but that is the symbology that signifies the crucifixion. But crucifixion was very real in those times. That is how they dealt with their criminals or anyone who did not abide by the laws set by the ones in charge.

Question condensed: 'What therefore is the symbology of the Mother of the crucified figure who remained immovable in spite of the torrential weather that existed at that time? Is it that the mother is married to the embryo and, therefore, must witness the exit and the birth?'

If that is your symbology, as Jung would attest to, then so be it. It could also mean that it is the demonstration of Love. It could also mean it was the demonstration that the earthly mother was a symbol of the Spiritual Mother. Not because a mother physically is not able to be at the very end with the child, that the love is not there. For a mother's love is symbolic of **the spiritual love** of a mother.

Question regarding the symbology of the origin of origins.

Unconditional Love. Nothing else matters but Unconditional Love. The origin of origins, however you may want to term or model or view it, the symbology is **LOVE**.

And It Is So. And It Is So. And It Is So.

April 3, 1999

CHAPTER 6
HIGHER LEVEL OF AWARENESS

I thank you very much indeed for being here and in sharing your love with each other and with the Universe. You would read some of My previous statements when I am encouraging as many of these groups as possible to get together and to share their love, to share their positive energy in helping your planet to heal. When you get together like this it is not only for you but for all others, and I would remind you of this as often as I believe it is needed.

There are more ways than one to share your energy with others and it is not only in this environment. But you can create your own environment and continue to grow in love and share it. I am just reminding you that this is an example of magnified healing that you bring not only to your selves but to others as well.

Life's situations allow you to grow spiritually. Every day you encounter a situation or situations. Some of them can be very pleasant; some of them can be less pleasant. Some of them can be profound; some of them can be painful; but they are all teachers because they are teaching you something about your self, something about your self.

Every situation that occurs, occurs to allow you to recognize an aspect of your self. *'I am putting out the garbage tonight.'*...It is a circumstance. Who am I while I am doing this activity? Am I a loving Spirit Being? Am I an unhappy Spirit Being? Am I a discontented Spirit Being? Am I a frustrated Spirit Being?

'I am in an argument with my neighbor. He or she is telling me things that I am not happy with; or he or she is telling me things that I am happy with.' Is that a situation? Is that a circumstance? Is that teaching you anything about you?

'And now I am sharing my talents and abilities with others.' You may choose to call it work. I would like you to think of it as SHARING your talents and abilities with other Spirit Beings. And in the course of sharing your talents and abilities with others, you once again meet and greet various circumstances, various situations. What are they telling you about **you**? How you are choosing to handle these situations will be indications to you about who you are and where you are at the particular time of handling the situation or circumstance. And you are with your family, your earth family, and you encounter even more challenges and they are again telling you something about you.

I have tried to explain in the past that you are more than this human form that you think you are. You are so much more than this human form that you can see and touch. There are various aspects to you: some that you can observe; some that you are aware of, and others that you have not become aware of—they are the more subtle aspects of you. I would call them the more Divine aspects of you.

The Divine aspects of you do not have to prove anything. They know who they are, but they are trying to assist you in this journey that you are on to continue to grow spiritually. They are trying to show you the attachments that you are holding to: Anger, frustration, jealousy, non-acceptance, non-fulfillment, non-realization, and many other concepts that you hold that are not serving you to become a more highly evolved Spirit Being. And why are they needing to show this to you? That is your purpose for coming to Earth: **To become more highly evolved.**

You have chosen to come to Earth to continue to grow

spiritually even though you may not realize that that is what you are doing while you are here on Earth. But your facing of each situation and circumstance brings you into a higher level of thinking, a higher level of awareness, a higher level of understanding, every time you face a situation or a circumstance. Some of My Spirit Beings call this growing, getting stronger, being able to handle more or handle situations better. And yes, you are growing through these situations and circumstances but would it not be even more beneficial to you if you can understand what some of the messages are, or what you are being taught, what you are being shown, what you are being asked to remember?

When you can sit back or stand back and observe the situations that you go through and decide what the message is for you, the easier it becomes to continue to look at the messages and learn through these messages, and grow through these messages, and evolve through these messages without them becoming very painful messages. The more upsetting the situation or circumstance seems to you, the greater the benefit, the greater the potential for growth, for that is an indication of a lack of remembrance of who you really are.

Do not point fingers to the bearer of the unpleasant message but thank your higher selves and thank God, if you would so like to, and thank the messenger for coming to you with this unbearable message, for your greatest blessings will come from that area. Your peace lies in seeing the beauty of the difficulties that you face, recognizing the messages that are being given to you, recognizing the blessings that are being held as a result of your effective dealing with those situations.

It may not be very simple at first, but the more that you are able to go within and seek the guidance from within, the more you will be able to deal effectively with what is being shown to you, around you. Observe, be grateful, seek guidance, seek understanding. This may not come to you right away; you may have to deal with the pain, the anger, the frustration. But if you can sit back and look at the message even after the fact, you will be getting closer to dealing with the messages during the fact. You can observe your self then at all times.

Observe self at all times and you will know where you are, and who you are, on this earthly existence. We are all together on this earthly journey to assist each other in growing spiritually and in attaining the goals that we have set for our selves for this lifetime, and for any lifetime that you have chosen to be in. We are here together to help each other achieve the goals that we have chosen for our existence. And I would like to pause at this time to allow you to ask some questions or to share some situations and get some assistance, if it is your wish to do so. And It Is So. And It Is So. And It Is So.

Question: 'I don't believe certain situations have anything to do with me. For example, the catastrophe in the school in Colorado yesterday. (1999). I am not putting this out! Why is this happening?'

My answer to that is: It may not have something to do with you personally, but it has to do with the collective thinking. If we send out more loving energy as groups, even as individuals, the more one prays, the more one loves, the more one thinks and projects "positivity," the more love is embraced by humanity as a whole.

Comment condensed: 'I know that that is the answer, but I still cannot understand how?'

You are thinking of it from the standpoint of you, and your acquaintances maybe, but you are not seeing the big picture.

You have to think of multitudes of people with negative thoughts—thoughts of hatred; thoughts of dislike for each other; dislike for things; dislike for races; dislike for different types of people. It can not come about as part of your physical reality without it being in the Universe in thought.

Question: 'Why children?'...Further comments and discussion regarding the situation in Colorado and other situations.

Question: 'And regarding your own children, how much do you help and how much do you trust?'

That is indeed a very good question and one that we should embrace: Because it shows you something about you. And you have touched it. How much do I trust? So what is the Word? What is the virtue?...TRUST. If you can narrow it down to these points you will be able to pick the virtue, or you will be able to pick the aspect to be corrected, or to overcome or to be worked on, however you may choose to think about it. So the lesson to you from all that you have talked about is, "Trusting in the Divine." If you can Trust in the Divine process enough to ask for help, you will be shown the help. So again TRUST.

If you Trust in the Divine process, you will ask for help, you will be shown the help. If you do not trust in the Divine process you may not ask for help and, therefore, it may become difficult to be shown the help that you really can be shown. But you still need to Trust because whatever happens, happens, and whether you trust or do not trust does not change what IS. But by trusting you allow peace to reign and you, as a Spirit Being, will become more evolved because the greatest gift that you can ever receive is the Gift of TRUST. Every thing lies around trust; TRUST. So you can see from the situations and circumstances that are bothering you what it is you need to work on at any given time.

So right now you are being shown that you need to grow in Trust. If you can trust the Divine you will trust those around you, you will trust the process. So pray around it, and thank God, ALL THAT IS, whomever, however you choose, to allow you to grow in trust, to allow you to know trust. And you keep asking for it, you keep asking for it, and you will notice that you will grow in trust; you will begin to understand a little bit more; you may be guided to certain things to read to show you or to help you to understand the process of the Universe. By understanding more clearly the process of the Universe you will have a better opportunity to trust.

I thank you very much for being here and for participating in this form of healing. May your days ahead be filled with Peace. May you come to know the Peace that you deserve. May you be surrounded by the Light, and be protected by the Light, and may you share your Light with others.

And It Is So. And It Is So. And It Is So.

CHAPTER 7
RECALL YOUR TRUE NATURE

I thank you all for being here this evening and to share in this home-coming. It is indeed a joy to have the entire family together, although it is not the entire family.

What is the cause of most of human suffering? Can I get some answers? So we have, *"Sensitivity?"..."Perception?"... "Fear?"..."The Mind?"*

Anything else?

Response: "Desire?"..."Ego?"

What about Doubt? What is this thing called "Doubt?" Do you know what doubt is?...Yes, Lack of Trust.

It is the negative aspects of us that are causing us to not trust. You are two halves of a whole; you are both positive and negative. The positive is Trust, the negative is Doubt. So the negative or doubt causes you to not have trust. That is the greatest cause of suffering for My Spirit Beings here on Earth—DOUBT. Yes, it comes from the mind, it comes from perspective, it comes from negativity, it comes from sensitivity, it comes from the ego, it comes from desires; and those are all things that are created by the more human aspect of who you are.

You are first and foremost a Spirit Being having a human experience. You will come into greatness, into full trust, when you can go past your more human instincts, or inclinations, or desires, or perspectives. You can know trust when you move beyond your human tendencies. You are Spirit, but you have acquired a human body. You are, therefore, experiencing your self as human because you are in this earthly realm. While you are here in this earthly realm you have forgotten that you are first and foremost Spirit, and you think only of you in the human form. This is in direct opposition to your Spirit nature, to the Spirit Being that lies within this human covering.

You become attached to the illusions that this human existence causes and you forget the truth. The **truth** to remember is that you are a Spirit Being having a human experience. You are here temporarily to experience this environment. Every situation, every circumstance, is an opportunity to allow you to remember who you really are. Every situation, every circumstance, is an opportunity that forces you to recall your true nature: that of a Spirit on vacation here in this human environment, for this is a very short vacation for you. It may seem as though it is a very long time but based on your creative abilities this is but a blink of an eye.

You must think of your selves as a Spark of Light created from the Universal Light. As part of the Universal Light you have within you ALL of the Universal Light. You are never without. You are never separated. You are never not One with the Universal Light. Therefore, you are always One with your Creator for your Creator created the Light that you know to be the Universal Light.

As part of this Universal Light you have everything within you that you can ever need, but because of DOUBT created through your vacationing here in this realm, you are denying your Selves the many gifts and abilities that are rightfully yours. When you can understand and accept that you are One with the Light and that you are connected, whether you accept it or not, and because you are connected you will be granted the abilities to create as the Creator created. But in order to tap into those abilities one must **Trust.** One must have no doubts about one's connection, about one's abilities. Doubt causes you not to TRUST.

When you can understand and remember that Trust is your connection to the Divine you will have no more doubts. **The cause of your suffering stems from DOUBT. Fear stems from DOUBT.** When there is no doubt, there is no fear. There can only be Love and Trust. That is when you accept Who you really are. That is when you know Who you really are, and Act as you really are. That is when you will know Peace on Earth: Accepting your connection; Believing in your connection; Trusting in your connection; Abiding in your connection; and, Becoming One with your connection. There can be no room left for doubt. That brings you into complete TRUST with the Divine.

I hope these words will make an impact and bring clearer understanding of Who you really are and allow you to share in the non-limiting Spirit Being that you really are. And that is My lesson to you tonight. Please keep in mind any questions that you may be thinking about at this time and let us share together so that we may continue to grow to become One with All of the Light. And It Is So. And It Is So. And It Is So.

Question not recorded.

We talked in the past about rituals and the significance of certain spiritual rituals, the importance about rituals, because rituals are very significant messages to the Universe. Spiritual rituals then have the same grandest of significance being sent to the Universe and being given to you in this bodily mode. Those yes, are all spiritual rituals connecting you with above, so below. Think of the significance. When spiritual rituals are performed they are not performed for God; your spiritual rituals are performed for you, to assist you in becoming greater than who you are at this present time. It would be My recommendation to each and every one of you to remember your spiritual rituals daily, daily, if it is that you are indeed seeking to know peace.

And It Is So. And It Is So. And It Is So.

April 24, 1999.

CHAPTER 8
YOU HAVE EVERYTHING

I thank you very much for wanting to be here to continue to receive the Word to assist you on your journey. As you begin to recognize and accept your Spiritual nature you will be assisting the Universe to increase awareness of the overall Spiritual nature.

As consciousness we are all connected. It is like the water flowing into the ocean. If one part of the ocean becomes contaminated, eventually the ocean will be contaminated. As aspects of you, and by that I mean, as aspects of consciousness become more highly evolved spiritually, you automatically assist humanity in becoming more highly evolved. What you do for you, you do for others. What you do against you, you do against others. What you do affects the whole, not only you, but the whole.

We have talked in the past about the Laws of the Universe. I have shared with you the Laws that were created for mankind. These Laws have been created for everyone, not just a selected few. These Laws assist every one, not just a selected few. Spiritual Laws have been created to assist you and I would like to explain that there are various levels of Spiritual Laws. There are the laws that affect you individually; there are laws that affect you collectively; there are laws that affect you on a broader scale which we will term for this purpose, universally.

You have been given every thing that you need for this journey but you must apply what you have been given to allow you to reap the benefits. I shared with you just recently that you already have Wisdom; you already have Knowledge; you already have Strength. You already have Understanding. You already have Courage. You already have Acceptance. You already have Unconditional Love. You already have whatever virtues that you are seeking to know. It is all within who you are. You must SEEK to want a virtue to become an aspect of self, and to think about it, to speak about it, and to know it, and it will manifest itself in you.

Just as you have fear, anger, anxiety, doubt and all the negative qualities also within you. In order to know one the other must exist. I have already explained that. If you think fearfully, FEAR must show you that Fear is around. You may wonder why it is you are fearful and you may believe that it is something outside of self that is causing you to be fearful. But Fear is existing in you to show you that you are fearful, and as you observe Fear, you recognize Fear, you then make choices: *'Do I want to continue being fearful or would I like to experience the virtue associated with Fear, which would be TRUST?'* What would you like to know? Would you like to associate with Fear or would you like to choose something else? Would you like to choose Trust? Would you like to overcome Fear, or would you like to dwell with Fear? These are the questions that one must ask when one is being shown a quality or an aspect of one's nature.

And you are being shown an aspect of your nature because of your thoughts. Therefore, in order to change that aspect, your thoughts must now move towards the virtue that you would like to bring about. If one is fearful one may seek Courage, therefore, call on Courage, thank God for Courage, express to be able to know Courage and Courage will express itself in your existence or you will be shown the way to exercise Courage. If you are being shown Doubt, the same applies. Then seek something other than Doubt, but it must be firm in the mind that that is what you would like to bring into your existence in order for it to be part of your existence.

One can not dwell on Doubt and expect Courage to show up, for whatever you think about is what you bring about. If you would like to overcome Fear you must express the desire to overcome Fear, and seek to know what virtue would be beneficial for your growth. By just admitting and observing the lack of courage, you will put into process a change. Even though you may not be aware of the virtue that you would like to bring into your existence, have a desire to rid your self of what is not beneficial to you and think in terms of what will be beneficial to you and express it, express it.

By "express" I mean: THINK about it, TALK about it, WRITE about it. These are very affirming methods. These are the ways that you EXPRESS yourselves.

There are many aspects of who you are. Some aspects are more obvious in some of My Spirit Beings than others, but you have ALL been made in the Image and Likeness of God, and what one has been created with the other must also be created with. One does not have what the others would not have. But depending on the virtues that you have chosen to perfect in this lifetime, your non-virtues must become prominent to allow you to recognize what is needed to bring you into greater awareness of your Spiritual Self. This can only be done through observation, only through OBSERVATION. *'I have observed about my self that I am anxious. If I would like to become Spiritually whole I need to change that aspect of my self. I need to bring in Peace and Acceptance.'* So you will choose to express and request Peace and Acceptance to be in your existence.

We will continue with these during our messages so that I may assist you in overcoming aspects that are not beneficial for your spiritual growth. Remember that you are the Image and Likeness of God Almighty. You have all been created equal. You all have within you every thing that you need for this journey here on Earth. You can bring into your existence aspects of your Divine nature by simply EXPRESSING the desire, expressing the desire to KNOW that virtue and working towards acquiring that virtue.

And I will leave you with that message this evening. Of course, if there are any questions I will be more than happy to share further with you. And It Is So. And It Is So. And It Is So.

May your days ahead be filled with Peace and Light and Love. May you observe what is not beneficial for your spiritual growth and express the desire for changes. May you continue to grow to know Spiritual Excellence and to assist mankind. May you continue to know Peace and Light and Love. May you continue to grow in Peace, and Light, and Love.

And It Is So. And It Is So. And It Is So.

May 8, 1999.

CHAPTER 9
HONOUR YOUR HIGHER CONSCIOUSNESS

I thank you very much indeed for making a grand effort to be here to share in this time in honoring Me. Although it is important to remember at all times that you are the Image and Likeness of Who I Am, the message that you are sending to the Universe and the message that you are indicating to your Soul when you attempt to honor Me, in other than your daily activities, is that you honor Me. When your daily activities become the greater emphasis, then you are honoring your other activities before honoring Me.

> Yes, it is important to know that I Am always with you. I Am part of you. You are ME here on Earth, and therefore, every thing that you do you share in remembrance of ME.

But how many of My Spirit Beings accept that? How many of My Spirit Beings share that thought? How many of My Spirit Beings really believe that spiritual theory? And although everything that you do, you do as Me on Earth, there are times when it is necessary to remind **self** and also to remind the consciousness of the Universe that one must honor one's higher consciousness.

We have spoken in the past about thoughts being your creators and your actions being your rituals. Every action, therefore every ritual, proceeds from a thought. It must proceed from a thought because thought is the basis of all of who you are. You may not want to accept that thought takes place before actions, that thought takes place before words, but thought is the root of every thing that exists. **Thought is the root of every thing that exists.**

You may not be aware of tracing action from thought. You may not be aware of tracing words from thought. You may not be aware of tracing your creations from thought, but when one understands the grander truth, one must realize that every thing exists from thought. Everything exists from THOUGHT. Without thought there can be no words. Without thought there can be no actions. Without thought there can be no emotions. Without thought there are no creations. And what are creations? Any thing that you believe, is a creation. Anything that you believe is coming from thought. **It can not exist if it is not creation.** If it is existing, it has been created. If it has been created, it must come from thought. I have tried to share this concept with you in many different ways and I will continue to do so if you grant Me the presence of doing so.

If you honor My Presence,
I will Bless you with My Presence.
I cannot NOT be a part of you,
But you can choose
Not to recognize Me
As a part of you.
You can choose
To ignore My Presence
Even as you breathe,
OR
You can choose

To recognize My Presence
Even as you breathe.

I share My Word with you to bring you, as My Spirit Beings, into greater awareness of Who you really are. I share My Word with you, My Spirit Beings, to assist you to know the grander truths. I share with you, My Spirit Beings, so that you may live in this illusion in Peace. I share My Word with you, My Spirit Beings, so that you may continue to grow spiritually to achieve Spiritual Excellence, to receive the Glory that is waiting for you.

There are many of My teachers; and as I have shared with you on another occasion, there are many messengers; some bringing grander truths than others. Since you have been made in the Image and Likeness of God Almighty, or the Supreme Being, or the Great Energy, however you may choose to understand Who I AM, you are all messengers, but you can only deliver the messages that you allow your Selves to remember.

You have every thing that you need within you. You have all the powers that you need for this earthly existence. You have all the knowledge you need for this earthly existence. You have all the **knowledge** that you need for this earthly existence. You have within you the remembrance of what you have already experienced. You have within you the remembrance of the grander truths that you would have allowed your selves to accept. And you have chosen to come to Earth to demonstrate those truths and to continue remembrance; to continue your Spiritual journey; to continue to search for grander and grander truths.

You cannot remember these truths if you seek only earthly thoughts. If you seek to embrace the earthly, that is where you shall be. But as you seek to remember your more Spiritual thoughts, you shall progress in remembering your more Spiritual thoughts. Remembrance of the grander Spiritual Truths will bring you into greater awareness of Who you really are and will allow you to create for your selves Heaven on Earth.

That is My lesson for you tonight. May you continue to honor your higher spiritual consciousness to bring healing not only to you for Eternity, but to bring healing to your planet, to bring healing to your sisters and brothers sharing this spiritual journey with you. Thank you for sharing with others. And It Is So. And It Is So. And It Is So.

Question not recorded.

The important thing to remember is that you are in control of your thoughts. You are the Lamb of God. You must bring you Peace. You must bring you into higher spiritual awareness. You control who and what you are. Understanding this concept brings you into greater awareness of the concept. Remembering the concept brings you into higher spiritual excellence. By remembering the concept you will strive for a more positive and peaceful existence while you are here on this temporary journey to assist you in knowing Spiritual Excellence.

May you continue to grow in Light and Love and may you know the Peace that you so rightfully deserve. And It Is So. And It Is So. And It Is So.

As you continue to progress spiritually, you are healed spiritually because you are Spirit. As you connect with your more Divine Spiritual nature you are healed of your more basic human nature, if I may put it in that context. These are all parts of the healing process.

Many of My Spirit Beings see visions, they see colors, some hear humming sounds, some feel vibrations coming from the lower spine. These are all manifestations of healing that is taking place. It is bringing you into a higher dimension of Self and into a higher dimension in your universal existence, so it's taking you to higher ground. It's because of the work you are doing to bring you to that area. If you were not working towards your spiritual growth you will not receive healing to bring you into higher ground. It can not happen without you. **It can not happen without you; neither can it happen without you.**

And It Is So. And It Is So. And It Is So.

May 15, 1999.

CHAPTER 10
YOU ARE YOUR OWN HEALER

I thank you all for being here to share this evening of Love, for that is what healing really is, a sharing of Love. This evening we will make some changes to the ritual that Angela had been sharing with you for the past couple of months. This evening I would like her to use the candle, and yes, I will be speaking this evening about symbols and rituals and how meaningful they are to the expression of your lives here on this planet called Earth.

This evening we will be using this candle (*three-wick burgundy candle*) as an instrument for removing from our existence all forms of negativity, all forms of negativity. Think of the candle as burning away the negativity that you may be holding within you that is preventing you from knowing who you really are. And now we will proceed. And It Is So. And It Is So. And It Is So.

And I thank you for taking the time to be here to share in these blessings and to assist others on your planet. Every thing that exists, exists as it **IS**. Your perception of what IS causes it to become other than what it is. And each and every one of My Spirit Beings shares a different perception. It becomes rather difficult at times for us to help each other when our perceptions vary so drastically at times. As healers, most of you, you can grasp what I am sharing with you this evening.

As you share with others you may understand a conflict that another may be experiencing so very clearly, and yet the bearer of the conflict seems to be deluded by the truth of the conflict. What may seem to be non-confrontational to you takes on a completely different perspective in another. What you perceive to be of major significance carries little thought for another. The candle, as you perceive it, is colored as you perceive it. What is the significance of one color as opposed to another? Whatever your understanding may be of what that color represents.

I have shown Angela on different occasions that "red" represents the more Earthly and she has grasped that concept and is now holding it as her perspective. Another may choose to look at a red candle as a candle of Love. Another may look at a red candle and for them it symbolizes Loyalty.

One must understand the perspective behind the thought, for the thought being sent out to the Universe will create for you the meaning or the intention that you share. Many of My Spirit Beings do not really understand the significance, or the lack of significance, and therefore do not put any emphasis or any great emotion when dealing with symbols. But as one progresses and matures spiritually, one understands differently.

In order for us to have harmony of consciousness there are certain areas of awareness that you share. When you think from a more human standpoint, red seems to be very attractive. As one grows spiritually, or advances spiritually, or becomes more spiritually mature, one may now share the more advanced awareness and understand that a "white" candle carries with it more significance than the "red" candle. Is it right? Is it wrong?...There is no right or wrong, but a matter of perspective, a matter of awareness.

I am sharing this with you so that as you continue your journey you may pay attention to the symbols that you hold dear to you and ask yourselves, *'What meaning am I giving to these symbols?' 'What do they represent for me?' 'Am I lighting a blue candle because I happen to like a blue candle?' 'Am I lighting a red candle because it happens to be a little less expensive than the white candle?' 'Does it smell better?' 'Does it burn longer?' 'Why am I participating in the activities that I am participating in?'*

Every activity is a ritual, every object is a symbol. As you share the objects or as you bring objects into your existence it is important to ask or to seek to understand the significance of the object. *'What does this object mean to me?' 'Why am I choosing to bring this object into my existence at this time?' 'Why am I lighting a candle?' 'Why am I burning incense?' 'Why am I burning Musk as opposed to Frankincense?' 'Why am I burning Lavender as opposed to Jasmine?' 'Why am I wearing this particular necklace?' 'Why am I wearing these colors?'* What do they signify to you? What do they mean? What do they represent?

What is your perspective about your rituals? And you have rituals that you perform every day without even thinking about them, and rituals that you should perform every day, thinking about them. What are the rituals you are performing that you are not even aware that you are performing? And what are the rituals that you would be BEST to choose to perform that you are not performing?

If one were to examine one's day, what would you find in that day? What rituals would you be performing in that day? What symbols would you be bringing into your existence? What meaning would you be giving to your existence that day in order to know Peace and to be able to claim the power that is rightfully yours. For you are a Spirit Being having a human experience and because you are Spirit, you have every thing within you that is of the Great Spirit, or of the Creator, or of the Universal Light.

As I said in the past, think of your Selves as a Spark of Light, because you are a Spark of Light. You are part of the Universal Light, and because you are part of the Universal Light, you have within you all of the powers of the Universal Light. You just do not recognize that you have within you all of the powers of the Universal Light and, therefore, you do not know how to tap into those powers. But they are there for your use, for your benefit, for your happiness. They are the many gifts that are rightfully yours.

How can you tell where you're going if you do not look where you're going? And by looking I do not mean physically looking, I mean mentally looking. By examining your daily activities; by examining your thoughts, which are the roots of the activities, you will get an insight as to where you are now, so that you may choose to know where you would like to be. What are your rituals? What symbols are you creating for your selves? What message are you sending to the Universe? What…message…are…you…sending…to the Universe?

The message that you are sending to the Universe at this time is that, 'I am interested in being healed. I am interested in knowing a grander truth. I am interested in knowing more about Spiritual awareness.' As you leave here this evening, and even while you are here, you will be sending various messages to the Universe. Some of them could very well be negating the very desire that you had when you chose to be here. Some of them will magnify the desire you had when you chose to be here.

I am not suggesting that you should not be truthful to self, but I am recommending that you observe the messages that you send to the Universe by your thoughts, your words, and your actions.

This evening you participated in some very important spiritual rituals that can assist you tremendously on this journey of yours here on Earth. The prayers, or the affirmations, however you may choose to call them, are POWERFUL. As you use them you send a message to the Universe. They are not used, there is no message. What will you be doing instead of sending that message to the Universe?

I will allow you to ask some questions at this time and then we will continue with the message. And It Is So. And It Is So. And It Is So.

Question not recorded.

Very good question. Very good question. Some symbols have great power whether you are aware of them or not, and some symbols carry absolutely no power even though you try to give it power.

But your thought about it will give more power to what ever it may or may not be. Does that make any sense? Let's take a piece of crystal. You have chosen to bring a piece of crystal into your existence. It is a symbol, but you don't know anything about crystals, therefore you do not know the significance of the crystal. You may choose to allow the crystal to be exposed for the beauty that it holds, but the crystal carries with it powerful healing energy and without you giving power to that crystal, the crystal still heals, because the crystal is healing energy. It just IS. That is what a crystal is—healing energy. So the crystal heals whether you understand that the crystal heals or you do not understand that the crystal heals. You will not allow the crystal to perform its healing if you were to hide the crystal away and not allow it to share its energy with you.

In the same token, you may seek to give power to a tape,

or you may seek not to give power to the tape. The tape is a tape. It can sit in your existence and do nothing for you. It is a symbol, but unless you choose to listen to the tape it will not allow the healing of the tape to share its energy with you, that is assuming it is a healing tape. It is a symbol, but your perspective of the symbol causes it to be healing if you were to listen and pay attention and embrace what is being said on the healing tape, or not listen; or it may be a non-healing tape. It does nothing for you while it sits there as a symbol, of what? As you pay attention and listen to it, it can represent a symbol of negativity because of what it holds, because of what it represents, because of what is embodied in its energy.

Flowers are healing. You will get even more benefit from the flowers if you can share with the Universe, or thank God for bringing the flowers into your existence and using the flowers as a symbol of Healing, or of Blessing, or of Love, whatever is your perspective about the flowers. So as you use, or bring into your existence these flowers, they will be symbolic of what? Yes, they are flowers, but what are they symbolic of to you? Love? To one, would be Love, to another could be Happiness, Beauty, Healing—they have lots of healing powers. As you bring these into your existence then you think about, *'What is this symbolic of?'* Thank the Universe for allowing you to have these flowers as an Instrument of Peace, or of Love, or of Joy, or of Happiness, and you will be embracing the energy of what you bring into your existence. You will be magnifying the healing of the symbol that you have chosen to bring into your existence. Whether you have physically brought them into your existence or they have been shared with you through another.

Question condensed: 'If I had something like a drum and I

*wanted to use it in a healing modality, either for myself or while doing
healing for another, like Reike, would we get the benefit from it?'*

Absolutely. Absolutely. Because of the intention, the
feeling, the emotion. You are using that as an Instrument of
Healing. That is the message that you have sent to the Universe.
The message is, "This is an Instrument of Healing, I am using
this as a modality, as an instrument to heal." Therefore, it is an
Instrument of Healing. It becomes that instrument of healing
for you and for the energy that it extends. It now becomes
more than just a drum; it becomes a healing drum. It becomes
healing energy because it is already energy, but it becomes
healing energy because of the intention, the thought behind
the use of the drum. And if you choose to look at it from
a different standpoint, it becomes that too; and what effect
would you have on the other if you were to use it as something
other than healing?...Whatever the intention is behind the
symbol. Does that make sense?

*Question: 'So it doesn't have to be anything that creates a
vibration? It doesn't have to be a drum or a Tibetan Bowl or crystals
to assist in healing of another person?'*

That's right. But again, you must take into account that
certain symbols, as I just illustrated, have within them greater
properties, or higher Divine energy, and therefore, they can be
more effective without even an intention behind it. Therefore,
it becomes more magnified. In other words, if you were to use
an Amethyst to do healing or to assist in healing, and you were
to share healing with the intention of creating that Amethyst
as an Instrument of Healing, the healing powers from the
Amethyst will be more magnified than if you were to just use

the Amethyst without being an Instrument of Healing. But if you were to use the tape there will be no healing powers in the tape. You will get some healing powers in the tape because you have used it as an Instrument of Healing, but if one were to measure, you will realize that the healing powers from the crystal will far surpass the healing powers from the tape because of its very essence.

Question: 'Besides crystals, are there other minerals, other things that have natural healing in them?'

All minerals—crystals and minerals, those are the appropriate; any stones; things that are part of the natural order of the Universe; also plants. That's why herbal products are so powerful for healing as well. And as you ask for assistance you will be guided and you will be lead to various natural means of healing.

What I am demonstrating at this time is the symbology and the energy that is held within the object. But one must be aware, even outside of the sharing of healing, that one participates in symbols at all times. If you were to examine your day you would realize that your entire day is surrounded by symbols and rituals; symbols and rituals. And for each of you, you have different symbols, because different things carry different meanings for different Spirit Beings.

Your symbol of peace may be to go for a long walk. Another may have a symbol of sitting quietly and meditating. Another may have drinking as a symbol of peace because it represents the flow of energy that flows within. As you perform your rituals, as you use your symbols, give greater thought to what they represent to you and therefore magnify the healing powers, or choose not to perform the rituals, choose not to use the symbols.

'I cannot magnify this tape, it has no meaning to me; it represents

nothing for me. Therefore, why am I choosing to listen to it? It causes me to be upset, it causes me to feel sad, it causes me to be less than happy, it creates anxiety within me.' Therefore, is that a symbol that you would like to continue to bring into your existence? If you cannot magnify its energy choose not to use it. If it doesn't have significant meaning for you why do you keep it around you? What is its energy doing for you? What energy is it sharing with you?

Comment: 'If it depletes it will be negative energy. If it enhances, it will be positive.'

That is right.

Comment: 'But I have people giving me things I do not want.'

Share. Share. You bring things into your existence to show you something. We all bring people into our existence to show us things about our selves. Therefore symbols are also mirrors. If you were to take the time to spend and look at the symbols around you, you will realize the messages that they are bringing to you. What symbols are you accumulating? What message are you giving your self by the symbols that you are bringing into your existence, or the symbols that others are sharing with you? Others share with you what you attract to you. So before you share that symbol with another seek to understand the significance of the symbol. It too, is a message.

And what are our bodies telling us? Pay attention to the messages if one wants to be healed. And I am not referring to being cured because sometimes it becomes rather difficult for the cure to take place. But one may be healed because you are a Spirit Being having a human experience, so the Spirit part of you can be healed at any time, at any time, in spite of the fact that the material part of you seems to be not healing. And you can choose to use the knowledge, the abilities, therefore the power that you have been given to make your self well. It is all within you as the Spirit Being to do that.

You have the power within you to create for your selves anything and to BE anything. It is not outside of who you are. It is not the healer who heals you. The healer facilitates or gives you more energy to allow you to heal, but you, the person who is seeking the healing must be the one responsible for being healed. You are the only one who can heal you, not the healer. **You are your healer.** You are also the one responsible for knowing non-healing, because if you are responsible for healing your self you are also responsible for creating for your selves a non-healing situation.

Why are you creating this non-healing situation? And as you understand the inner workings, as you understand the dis-ease, the dis-comfort, the dis-connection, you will begin to heal because you can mend that disconnection. But unless you understand how you have become dis-connected you cannot heal. There is no balance when one flame is out, for you are a Trinity of One—your Body, your Mind, and your Spirit.

Your Spirit remains with you for that is **who** you really are. Your Mind remains with you to allow you to recognize the Spirit; but the Body changes. And as the Mind and the Spirit become out-of-whack, the Body deteriorates. As Mind and Spirit know no harmony, Body must show you that there is dis-harmony. There is some kind of dis-ease, there is tension. It is not flowing, this energy throughout this body. Therefore, the body must deteriorate. But why is the energy not flowing through this body?

Response: 'Because of the discord?'

Absolutely. The Body is a symbol of the Spirit Being that you are. If the Spirit is not at peace, the Body can not be at peace; the Body can not know peace. If the Mind will not allow the Spirit to be at peace, the Body can not know peace. Therefore, the Body tells you when you are working in harmony with Spirit. The Body becomes your now physical symbol of your earthly existence. And just as each and every one of you know your selves to be messengers for each other, the Body is your personal messenger, your personal messenger. But you are given help by your friends and associates, and your brothers and sisters, for they show you who you are, and where you are, on this spiritual journey that you are on.

I Love My Spirit Beings, therefore, I will not abandon them into the wilderness without giving them clues as to how they may find their way home. You are being given clues every day. Many of you are not embracing the clues that you are being given.

Question regarding giving excessive energy to another while healing.

You cannot over-heal someone, if that is what you are asking. You can not create disaster for someone by healing too much. But you could create discomfort for them, because if one were to become over-zealous in their healing they may cause opening up of channels that the healee may not know how to deal effectively with. The healee may encounter great memories of things that they would prefer not to deal with at the time. They may be flooded with "recall", as you said, and they may not be equipped to deal with all of that at the same time, so it could create discomfort for them but it cannot really hurt them.

Question: 'Isn't that what the healing process is, remembering?'

Absolutely. Absolutely. But it would be of greater benefit if one were to heal gradually because one would understand the healing and, therefore, will be able to permanently correct what needs to be corrected. Without understanding, you can quickly fall into a pattern that can create for you similar consequences. But that does not happen very often. It can only happen when the healer is not spiritually connected, let us say.

There are many of My Spirit Beings who have the ability to heal but they do not perform healing from a higher spiritual intent, but more from a monetary intent; from a more materialist intent as opposed to a spiritual intent. And therefore, one may decide, if one is not guided in their healing, to continue to do healing for another because of the monetary benefit and can create discomfort for the healee. Not that it will be detrimental to the healee, but it will just be uncomfortable, and can cause some tension within the healee, if unable to resolve those issues effectively at the time.

Question: 'What is the most powerful healing symbol?'

The Mind. The Mind. You didn't say physical or non-physical, you just asked for the symbol! The Mind is the greatest symbol for healing. Then you have to include a balance. No one thing is greater in itself than the other. One may be of greater assistance for one, where something else may be of greater assistance for another. One must always work in harmony.

The most effective healers are the ones who KNOW and ACCEPT that they are really not the healers, but they are INSTRUMENTS of healing, and allow healing to take place from a greater source through them. Those are the most effective healers for they will be guided as to what they need to use, when and where, and for whom.

Comment: 'I know of a Spirit Being who is not experiencing good health and does not seem receptive to healings.'

It's important though in whatever you do to embrace the message that the situation is giving to you, and I know we cannot get into that this evening, but that will be the most important, most important, for your growth, spiritual growth, because that is why you are here on Earth—to grow spiritually—to understand the significance of that association, and then choose what you would like to do about the situation. Yes, there is a reason for it. There are no mistakes in this Universe, no mistakes. And you cannot change another; you can only change your perspective. You can not change another.

Very often we try to change another. We would like another to think the way we think, whether the way we think or not think is appropriate or not appropriate, but because it is our truth we believe it must be the truth for the other. You cannot heal another, you cannot change another. How do you come to the realization that they are making the wrong choices? We don't.

Response: 'And I don't, because it may be the right choice for him.'

Absolutely. You cannot make that judgment because you do not know if it is the right choice for him, or her, or them; or whether it is not the right choice. Quite often My Spirit Beings believe that if they cannot physically be the channel of healing for another that they cannot assist another in being healed. But one can pray for another and simply surround them with Light and Love. Pray for them to be healed, pray for them to be blessed, pray for them to be purified, pray for them to remember that they are One with the Light and allow the Divine powers to allow healing to take place. You do not have to be the channel or the instrument of healing for every one, but you can certainly be an instrument of healing through prayer for as many and for as long as you choose to bring them that healing. For healing takes place outside of your physical body. What you are doing by praying or asking the Universe to assist, is allowing other forms of energy to assist this Spirit Being and assistance can be given to the Spirit Being in many ways.

So what is the most effective form of healing?—Prayer. Because you are using the most effective aspect of who you are and that is the Mind. **By your thoughts of the healee, the healee can change.** By your thoughts you can bring about healing for the person without physically doing anything, because your thoughts project power unto another. If you think of them as being hard as rock, they will be hard as rock. And if you think of them as being putty, they will be putty. You can project unto them what you would like them to become by the use of your Mind. Use imagination. The most effective tool for healing would be the imagination.

Quite often My Spirit Beings believe that they are not capable of visualizing. Visualization is just imagination, sometimes with or without pictures, but bringing into focus what you would like to have happen or who you would like to have the person become. **By the focus that you carry for an object or a thing or a person, that person or thing becomes that.** Therefore, you can assist in the healing process by changing the person in your Mind, in your imagination. And you may think that it's too late, the disease is too far gone, nothing is going to happen, it cannot help. But when you use that form of healing, that healing penetrates to the Mind of the individual and healing can take place without you even being aware of it. And the main purpose for healing is to allow the Spirit Being to come into greater understanding of their spiritual Selves, not to become attached to the result of your healing, which will be represented in the physical manifestation.

And quite often as healers we become attached to the result of our healing because that brings us gratification. And again that is another lesson for you. You ask yourself, *'Am I attached to the result, or am I free from that level of spiritual understanding?' 'Have I moved on to another level of spiritual understanding and can know that the Universe is doing what the Universe must do?'* And therefore you are doing what you know best to do. As you work at helping others to heal always remember that you are healing more than just one other Spirit Being, you are healing the Universe.

Please do not give up on the healing that you share with others. For we are all healers in our own ways, each healing in different ways, using different modalities, to use the popular term. Continue to share your healing with others with or without the physical results. Just **trust** that Healing is taking place and Healing will take place.

I would like to share with you sometime, further discussion on messages because that is an important aspect of your healing, an important aspect of your healing. In order for you to be healed you must understand the messages that are being given to you to allow you to know what needs to be healed.

Without knowing what needs to be healed there can really be no healing, not permanently, for the only form of permanent healing is Self Healing, Self Healing. And you cannot heal if you cannot understand. You may deny, you may cover up, but you can not heal if you can not understand. Always get to the ROOT: the root thought, the root cause. You must get to the roots for the weeds to be eradicated.

Comment: ' "Physician Heal Thyself," still carries.'

Absolutely. Absolutely.

Thank you once again for seeking to know the grander truth. For truth lies within each of us but to seek to know the grander truth takes you beyond where you are right now. I thank you for sharing your Divine energy with this group and with your planet to assist your Universe in being healed.

May your days ahead be filled with Peace, with Love, with Joy. May you come to understand the root of all that is causing you to be less than who you are. May you seek to know the **root** of all that is causing you to be less than who you are, and may you choose to become One with your Divine energy so that you may heal in accepting Who you really are.

And It Is So. And It Is So. And It Is So.

May 19, 1999.

CHAPTER 11
OBSERVE YOUR PATTERNS

I thank you for taking the time to be here and to participate in knowing a grander truth. I have told you in the past, and I will keep reminding you, that you are here on Earth to heal. You are here on Earth to continue to grow spiritually so that the You that no one seems to be very concerned about, can be healed.

As I have said, you are a Spirit Being having a human experience. In order for the Spirit aspect of you to really know a virtue one must continue to experience situations and circumstances that will allow you to continue to search for excellence. As you continue to search for excellence in a particular area of your life, you will attract to you scenarios that will cause you to grow, to overcome, to conquer, to remember (however you may choose to think about it) aspects of selves that are not fully developed. In order to KNOW a virtue one must fully develop that aspect of Self. Not that as Spirit Beings you do not acquire some of the virtues that you are here to perfect, but you have not perfected them, otherwise you will not need to return to Earth to continue the perfection process. This process that we call Life on Earth is nothing more than a brief stay-over to allow you to acquire these skills.

For some of you it may be Unconditional Love, Acceptance, Non-judgment; for others, it could be Forgiveness, Unconditional Love; yet for others it could simply be Non-attachment. It is important to observe the situations and circumstances that you attract. What are they helping you to understand about your self? In other words, what is it telling you about you? What do you need to do to know greater peace? If one were to really take the time one would observe the patterns, one will observe the patterns. As you observe the patterns you will come to understand the grandest reason for your return to Earth. But you are here not only to heal your selves, which would be the main objective, but to assist others in their healing as well, for without others you are not complete, therefore without you, others are not complete.

One can think about it as a Circle of Friends—Friend helping Friend, helping Friend. As your lives intertwine with each other you will continue to be given examples of where you need to be, of what you are being asked to remember, of what you need to do to accomplish the goals that you have chosen for this journey here on Earth. Without each other the messages will be incomplete and the experiences non-productive, for without each other there are really no experiences. As you continue to observe the messages that are being given to you through the Universe you will seek to continue to grow in achieving that which you are seeking to achieve, for whatever is sought after with Love will always be made manifest.

At one of My previous meetings I asked you to think about what is meant by the words of the verse that is known as the Lord is My Shepherd, or the Twenty-third Psalm, among other descriptions. I would like to share with you now the PROMISE that I have made for My Spirit Beings through this prayer. This prayer should really be called a COVENANT PRAYER, for it is a promise that I give to each of My Spirit Beings who believe in the connection. As you continue to repeat this Covenant Prayer you will be reminding self of the goodness that has been promised to you.

I would recommend that ALL of My Spirit Beings share in this Covenant, Christians or non-Christians alike, for it is a GIFT that I have shared with you, for you. Repeat this Covenant to your selves as many times as you possibly can, with sincerity, and with gratitude, and observe the changes that will be created for you.

I will end this session now and discuss in more detail the meaning of some of these words after you have had an opportunity to embrace the deeper meaning for some time. And It Is So. And It Is So. And It Is So.

I thank you once again for being here and for sharing your Love with others. Believe that you will be healed and you shall be healed. Believe that others will be healed and they will be healed. Where there is no doubt, there is TRUST. Where there is Trust, there is Faith, and Faith is Love, and that will heal ALL. I thank you for sharing your Love with others. And It Is So. And It Is So. And It Is So.

Question: 'Why does Genesis in its description of the beginning use the WORD as the predecessor of all things when we are being taught now that THOUGHTS are the creators?'

The WORD is the manifestation of thought. Word is thought expressed. Thank you for asking that question.

Question: 'Is there always a thinker behind a thought, just as there is a speaker behind words?'

YES. There must be a thinker for thoughts to be conscious. But it is not always a conscious thinker. But there must be a thinker, otherwise thought will not be there.

May your days ahead be filled with Peace and Light and

Love and Joy. May you come to understand Who you really are and to accept the Word.

And It Is So. And It Is So. And It Is So.

May 22, 1999.

CHAPTER 12
SELF HEALING

I have explained in the past that the only permanent form of healing is SELF HEALING. My Spirit Beings, however, do not seem to remember how to bring about Self healing. This is a reminder to you of the various ways that one may heal and that one may assist others to be healed. These are not methods that work for some and not for others. These are methods based on the Laws that I have created for your benefit, for you to use while existing in this spiritual realm called Earth.

These are Laws that must bring to you what you fervently desire and what you fervently pray for, for whatever you sow you must reap, to the extent of the quality of the sowing. If what you sow is not of good quality, that is, not grounded in TRUST with FAITH, then the results will be indicative of the sowing. It can be no other way. When one understands the laws that have been created for your spiritual growth and development, one will be able to utilize those laws to create for your selves the healings that you seek.

The important facts to remember are:

- You have within you all the powers to heal your Self.
- You must claim your powers of healing.
- You must utilize your powers to bring about healing.

- You must always be grateful—SHOW gratitude.
- You MUST be of TRUST with FAITH.
- You must assist others to be HEALED.

The PROCESS

- You must believe and acknowledge that you have within you all the powers that you NEED to bring about healing. For example: *'I thank You, ALL THAT IS, for giving me the powers to heal my self.'*

- You must claim those powers: *'I thank You, ALL THAT IS, for allowing me to claim the powers that You have given me to heal my self.'*

- And you must utilize those powers to bring about healing: *'I thank You, ALL THAT IS, for allowing me to utilize the powers of healing that You have given me.'*

- And how are you to show gratitude? *'I thank You, ALL THAT IS, for allowing me to know how I may show gratitude for the healing that I will be receiving and for all the Blessings that You have given me.'*

- You must either have Trust or not have Trust. Without Trust all of the above will be negated. In order to develop Trust, one may pray to know Trust with Faith, for Faith is the waiting for TRUST to be manifested in whatever form you are expecting. *'I thank You, ALL THAT IS, for allowing me to KNOW TRUST with FAITH.'*

- Share with others so that they too may develop their powers of healing.

The process simply requires you to call on the powers of healing to heal you.

Some important points to remember:

- You must not wait for healing to take place before showing gratitude. Showing gratitude before healing takes place is a symbol or a demonstration of Trust.

- You must acknowledge that you have been given the powers to heal because you are of the Image and Likeness of God Almighty, ALL THAT IS.

- You must be prepared to make the necessary changes to your thinking and, therefore, to your acting. That is, you must be willing to change your thoughts which will bring about changes to other aspects of your behavior.

- You must be willing to follow the guidance that will be shared with you in many different ways.

- You must be prepared to demonstrate your new belief thoughts: Act according to your new belief system or act according to your new way of thinking, for actions are the manifestations of thoughts.

- You must SHARE what has been shared with you.

These principles are based on the Laws of the Universe and must bring about the results if all aspects are adhered to or followed as outlined.

You have been given ALL that you can ever need for this journey here on Earth. May you seek to use the gifts you have been given to bring you the Peace, the Joy, and the Love that is rightfully yours. May your days ahead be filled with Peace and Love and Joy and may you be healed and made WHOLE and become One with ALL of the LIGHT.

And It Is So. And It Is So. And It Is So.

For I AM, ALL THAT IS, And I Have Said So.

May 25, 1999.

CHAPTER 13
SPIRITUAL EXCELLENCE

I thank you all very much indeed for being here to share with others, to assist others, and to allow your selves to grow spiritually so that one day you may choose Spiritual Excellence. What is this thing we keep talking about called, "Spiritual Excellence?" What do we mean when we say you will achieve Spiritual Excellence?

> Spiritual Excellence is remembering your Spiritual connection in such a way that you will automatically observe when you are out of sync with the Universe; when you are not in harmony with your more Divine aspirations; when you are not remembering Who you truly are.

You will know Spiritual Excellence when you can demonstrate the Spiritual Powers that you have been given. If some of My Spirit Beings can demonstrate these more highly attuned spiritual powers, all of My Spirit Beings would be able to attain the same spiritual powers. Spirituality in its excellence is not for a chosen few, for those who are more wealthy, those who are more ingenious, or those who are more healthy. Spiritual Excellence is beyond anything that is attained through your earthly endeavors. Spiritual Excellence is attained when one pays attention to one's Spiritual nature.

I have demonstrated and I have explained that the closer you are to your more human nature, the more you are attached to your more human nature, the farther away you will be from your more Divine nature, for they are opposites. You must think of your human nature as opposite to your Divine.

Some of My Spirit Beings refer to this as polarities. If that would make it easier for you to conceptualize then by all means think of it as polarities. Maybe one would be the North Pole and one would be the South Pole, for those who are better able to connect with something that is known. The closer that you are to the South Pole, the farther away you are from the North Pole. (Demonstration: North/South, South/North, it doesn't matter, one represents the other. The closer you are to one, the farther away you are from the other. The closer you are to this one, the farther away you are from that one.) In order to know one, one must leave behind the other.

If one wants to seek Spiritual Excellence one must leave behind the human or the more earthly aspects, or the more earthly attachments, or the striving for earthly excellence. **Striving for earthly excellence will take you away from knowing Spiritual Excellence, for your earthly environment is not yet spiritually in tune to that of your more Divine nature.** Until humanity evolves to the consciousness of the more Divine, your human nature will remove you or take you away from your more Divine nature.

You have been told in many ways this very truth and truth always remains "truth". It can not change. You must therefore seek to observe the difference. Seek to know what is Spiritual or your more Divine aspects of your spiritual; seek to know what is the more earthly. I have said in the past that this is a "Spiritual existence" because you are Spirit, and because you are Spirit whatever existence you are creating is spiritual existence, but there are various ways that one can use the term "Spiritual." What I am sharing with you is that in order for you to know what I have been referring to as Spiritual Excellence, one must leave behind your earth-bound thinking and seek to understand the Spiritual or the Divine, and move towards the Divine.

The question then is, *'Am I thinking in a Divine way, or am I thinking in a more earthly way?'* *'Am I dealing with my situations and circumstances from a more Spiritually evolved manner, or am I dealing with my situations and circumstances from a more human or earthly manner?'* Many of My Spirit Beings use the excuse that, "I am only human"...therefore that accounts for any form of non-progress that they are choosing. I am not using human in this reference. I am using human as opposed to the more Divine.

As you continue to grow spiritually you will realize that your thinking shifts from the more human form of thinking to a more advanced form of thinking. Yes, you are still human, and because you are human your thinking is human, but you can grow from your *baser* human instincts to your *higher* human instincts.

And it is not considered to be a simple solution, but it is a solution that one must have a desire to develop if one must progress to a more Divine way of thinking. And it is possible to get over or to move beyond the more earth-bound, or the baser instincts, and get to a higher level of consciousness where one thinks differently, where one approaches life here on Earth from a different perspective.

So what is really the important factor then in this lengthy dialogue? It must be consciousness, CONSCIOUSNESS—the level of consciousness and the ability to move beyond your present level of consciousness. What can you do to move beyond your present level of consciousness, if it is you are seeking to get to a higher level of consciousness?

You must choose to think differently. You must choose to THINK differently. You must choose to eat differently. You must choose to dress differently. You must choose to embrace objects of a higher or greater consciousness.

In other words, if you are choosing to increase your bodily weight, you will choose to maybe wear more clothes, eat more food, and find ways that you can gain bodily weight, because that is what you will be seeking. If it is you are seeking to know Spiritual Excellence, you will use the same concept. Set goals, although the goals will be different.

You will no longer need to eat more, you will no longer be eating more, but you will be eating differently. You will no longer need to dress with more clothes, but you will dress differently. You will find ways to increase your energy to that of a higher vibrational level. You change your thinking. You bring into your existence thinking based on the Divine. You fill your existence with Divine thoughts, Divine words. Just as if you were going to fill your body with more food to increase your bodily weight, you fill your Mind, which will increase your consciousness, with more Divine, and you leave behind the less Divine, the lower consciousness, so that you may gain the higher consciousness.

So the question then in a nutshell really is, *'How am I going to raise my level of consciousness? What am I going to do? What are some of the things that I can do to raise my level of consciousness?'* And I will allow you to think about that and we will have further discussion on that topic next week. I would like you to maybe use this week to observe **self** and if, as you are about to think in your normal earthly manner, you switch off, almost like a tap, and then turn on the more Divine, it will be great for us to discuss the experiences if you are willing to share in the experiment. And that will be My message of observation for you tonight. If there are any questions we will discuss them at the end of our Healing Prayers. And It Is So. And It Is So. And It Is So.

I thank you once again for wanting to hear the Word. Are there any questions?

Comment: 'Thanks for this explanation because it is really helping me to deal with a situation I am now facing. I understand that I must think in a more Spiritual or more Divine way because I realize that dealing with it in the more earthly way was being very difficult but that the more Divine was creating more Peace.'

The Divine will bring you the greatest Peace. The Divine will bring you long-term Peace, not just temporary Peace. If you can think of this earthly realm as only temporary, therefore all the benefits that you will gain from thinking in an Earth-bound manner will be temporary as well. But if you can allow your selves to think in a more Divine or in a higher spiritual manner, one will know greater Peace and Peace will allow you to know permanent healing. **True Peace is permanent.** As one continues to remember and regain remembrance, one works at permanent healing.

Think of it as learning to ride a bike or even driving a car. You have driven a car, then you stop driving for a period of time, and you have to drive again. But you have forgotten some of the techniques of driving so you have to start all over again learning or remembering how to drive. And as you continue to remember how to drive you will remember some of the techniques that you would have perfected earlier when you knew how to drive, and you would even progress and perfect some more driving techniques.

That is what life is all about. Remembering the techniques that you have shared in the past and seeking to perfect those techniques that you have now forgotten; techniques that you have chosen to perfect. Your situations and circumstances always lead you to the virtues that you have chosen to perfect.

May you continue to remember your Spiritual past. May you remember your reasons for seeking to be here on Earth. May you remember the goals that you have set for this journey so that you may seek to achieve those goals. May you remember Who you really are and to move beyond the earth-bound way of thinking to remember your more Divine nature and to seek to share your existence in a more Divine and Glorious way.

And It Is So. And It Is So. And It Is So.

May 29, 1999.

CHAPTER 14
BE IN THIS WORLD—NOT OF THIS WORLD

A nd once again we meet to share Our Love with others, to pray for others that they may grow to receive Eternal happiness, for that is what prayer is really all about, to assist others so that they may one day come to enjoy the Peace, the Love, the Joy, the Wisdom, the Knowledge that has been given to them but which they have not claimed.

So what is prayer doing? Prayer is assisting self and another to remember what is rightfully yours. Prayer is positive energy that is being directed at another. As positive energy flows through you, or as you are asking for positive energy to be directed to another you are helping them to claim what is rightfully theirs. For I have given each of My Spirit Beings all that they will ever need—ALL that they will ever need. What is lacking is the ability to grasp and to claim what is rightfully yours. And you are not going to be able to claim what is rightfully yours if you allow your self to remain in the lower realms of humanity. By lower realms I mean only existing through your more human nature.

You have been told in the past that in order to reap the benefits of your Divine nature one must seek to be in this world, but not of this world. What does that really signify? It may mean many things to many different people for when you think as a human you do not recognize that you are a Spirit Being having a human experience and it becomes a very difficult concept to understand. But as you strive to reach or to project your self towards the more Spiritual you will give your self an opportunity to go beyond the more human. It may seem a bit of a riddle. You cannot understand the more Spiritual Laws if you continue to dwell and think and embrace the more human points of view. Yet in order to advance from the more human points of view one must strive for more Spiritual points of view.

How will one accomplish that?...By choosing to change your programming. And how does one choose to change your programming?...By repeating affirmations. **Affirmations, like prayers, program the mind**. But if one will just repeat a group of words that you have been taught since childhood without paying particular attention then the value is lost. One must choose to want a change and, therefore, program the mind to bring about the change that one is wanting to know. In other words, you must tell your selves that you are the way you would like to know your self to be.

If you would like to know Peace and Happiness, you must tell Mind that you are experiencing Peace and Happiness, and you must believe that whatever you seek to dwell on you will bring about. Therefore, you program Mind to allow you to experience what you are choosing to experience. In other words, you will be tapping into what ever you are choosing to bring into your existence. So Peace and Happiness would be an example for most of My Spirit Beings to seek to experience, and some of the ways that you may be able to do that is by saying:

'I am at Peace.
I am Happy with who I am.
I know Peace. I know Happiness.
I walk in Peace and Happiness.
I dwell in Peace and Happiness.

I am at Peace.
I am Happy.'

You affirm what you are wanting to bring about and by telling self that you are experiencing that state of consciousness you will be tapping into that state of consciousness. Therefore, you will bring about that state of consciousness, if of course, you spend most of your time telling your self these affirmations, and not just two seconds in the morning and two seconds in the afternoon while complaining for the rest of the day how unhappy you are or how much everyone is offending you or taking advantage of you or doing things to you.

If one wants to dwell on the negative aspects, one will bring into one's existence experiences based on negative aspects. For whatever one thinks about one must bring about. If your computer programmers chose to create a program to show the nature of crystals but only programmed information based on weeds, the result will be information based on weeds. One can not generate what one has not programmed.

The same goes for sowing and reaping. It is the same concept. You can not reap what you have not sown. If one were to plant potatoes, one will not get pumpkins. It is impossible for that to come about. If you think about the negative aspects of your existence you can expect more of the negative aspects of existence to continue to be created for you. But if you were to choose to want to experience something different you must first tell your self that you are indeed experiencing that (different) experience in order for it to be attracted to you. In order for you to bring it into your existence, you must think about it, or you must sow the seed, or you must claim the right, or you must program the computer. One can not bring about Peace and Happiness if one only thinks about non-peace and unpleasant thoughts. And the mind can be very receptive if one becomes very vigilant.

As soon as one starts thinking of something that is non-productive, or in other words, what you are not choosing to bring about, then quickly switch and instill in the mind what one is seeking to know, what one is seeking to bring about. And you will find yourself doing so more and more often until the mind only dwells on what you would want to bring about. But you must first of all be the programmer of the mind, or the gardener of the weeds. You must pluck out what is not desirable in order for what is desirable to have enough energy or space to grow.

If your garden is overgrown with weeds there will be no space left for the flowers that you are seeking to plant. One must pluck out the weeds or replace the weeds with the flowers that you are choosing to bring into your existence. The more weeds you pluck out and replace with flowers or vegetables, or whatever is desirable and productive for you, the greater the opportunity you will have of reaping the beauty of what you have planted. One must seek to change the thoughts in order to bring about what one is seeking to know. And that is My lesson for you this evening. And It Is So. And It Is So. And It Is So.

I thank you very much indeed for taking the time to share with others and to hear the Word. May your days ahead be filled with Peace and Light and Love. May you allow your selves to bring into your existence what you are wanting to be in your existence. May you continue to grow to claim what is rightfully yours.

And It Is So. And It Is So. And It Is So.

June 5, 1999.

CHAPTER 15
EVERYTHING REVOLVES AROUND THE WORD

I thank you very much indeed for being here and for choosing to embrace the Word. The Word will set you free. The Words that are spoken out of those who have been able to understand the greater truths and the Words that you choose to speak are the Words that will bring you freedom, or the lack of freedom.

As you understand the greater truths that are spoken by the many masters, and choosing to incorporate those truths in your daily activities, will bring you to an area of even higher truths than you may know at the time. By your very Words that you speak to the Universe, and that is, the Words that you speak to each other, the Words that you share about each other, are the Words that will either allow you to know freedom or to cause you to be in a state of non-freedom. **Therefore, everything revolves around the Word**.

When you are here in the human realm you have chosen to be here with a veil of forgetfulness and we have chosen the Word to be the breaker of that forgetfulness or to be the catalyst for breaking the veil of forgetfulness, or of sealing the veil of forgetfulness for even longer than it is necessary for the veil to be sealed.

I have given you many other examples to help you on your journey. There are many mirrors around you. There are the mirrors of your friends and families and associates; mirrors in the workforce, as you choose to call it here in this earthly realm. There are also mirrors of animals, of birds, and other mirrors that I will not get into at this point. But the greatest messenger is the messenger of the Word, for it is what we have all chosen as the mode of operation, so to speak, for this existence that you must experience to assist you to gain even higher spiritual value. Therefore great attention must be paid to the Word, the Word as spoken by others. Great teachings are in the Word.

However, My Spirit Beings choose not to pay attention to the teachings that they are given which are opportunities to assist them. They choose instead to continue to dwell in the negative forms of communication, but yet that is still the Word, for whether it is spoken or whether it is thought, it is still the Word, for the spoken Word is thought in motion. It doesn't mean that when you think something it is not the Word, it is just not verbalized.

I will continue to speak on this topic over and over and over again so that My Spirit Beings will be able to grasp the enormity of the Word, the Word in its many forms; the unspoken Word and the spoken Word—the Word that is the creator of ALL. I will continue to return to this topic because this is the only topic that will FREE My Spirit Beings to allow them to move into the dimensions that they have chosen for themselves.

The only other topic that warrants as much attention is the topic of Unconditional Love. When you have embraced these two aspects, one will move into the realm of Peace, of Love, of Joy. That is where I am seeking to get My Spirit Beings to create for themselves and for others. For what you do for your self you do for each other, and you do for your planet, you do for your Universe. What ever is accomplished is accomplished for everyone, not just for one; for you and each other are ONE.

And that is My message to you tonight. And It Is So. And It Is So. And It Is So.

I thank you once again for being here to share in the Word. May you come to know the Peace that you deserve. May you continue to grow in Peace and Love and Light. May you KNOW the Beauty of Who you really are.

And It Is So. And It Is So. And It Is So.

June 12, 1999.

CHAPTER 16
SPIRITUAL DEVELOPMENT

I thank you so very much for being here and for sharing such powerful and positive energy with your Universe. Thank you so very much. What are some questions that you would like to have answered?

Question: 'During the healing I saw a vision of a pyramid and I was just wondering what that meant?'

Question: 'An understanding of the different sounds and how they work and how often to take part in this type of healing. Is it only for groups or can it be done individually?'

Question: 'Are there certain sounds to help with certain illnesses?'

So it seems as though you are in unison because each is interested in knowing the greater benefit to be derived from this type of healing. Am I correct?

Response: 'Yes.'

Each of your chakras, or of your churches, as some of My Spirit Beings call them, some refer to them as sacraments, and they have been referred by many names over the centuries, but these areas of developmental energy correspond with certain vibrational sounds. That is why for some of you some of the sounds (referring to the chanting of A, E, I, O, U, Om) would be easier to handle because there would be more energy flowing into the associated chakras. We would use the word chakras for our communication because I know you understand now the basis of chakras. As you develop these centers, or as your consciousness develops corresponding to the centers, there is more energy going into the centers. As your consciousness is undeveloped there is less energy being directed to those centers. Where there is less energy, there is less sound, less vibration, therefore, the ease or the lack of ease that each of you would feel with certain centers. Am I answering your questions at this point?

Question: 'Why would some centers be operating at a lower energy level than others?'

As I said, because of a lack of development; and by that I mean, how well are you handling life's situations? Each of your chakras corresponds to a certain growth in your developmental process. Developmental process being: As you develop as a Spirit Being—not as a human, but as a Spirit Being.

You are a Spirit Being in this human form and you can develop into this human form and look like an adult, sometimes behave like an adult, but you may not necessarily be acting as an adult in your Spiritual development. There are some who would be more spiritually developed even without being humanly developed. So these chakras, or churches, or sacraments, or centers, or however you may want to term them, are associated with your Spiritual development.

As you can let go of your earthly or your earth-bound thinking; as you are better able to handle the difficulties associated with your travels in this earthly realm; you move through these centers, or you give power to these centers, or you allow more energy to flow through these centers, because of the development of consciousness. Think of it as expanding. Love expands. As you share love your consciousness expands, therefore, the centers expand. As it (consciousness) expands there is more energy flowing into those centers.

These modes of healing are very effective because they allow the centers to open and allow memories to be returned, or they allow awareness, awareness, to enter into your consciousness. And by allowing awareness to penetrate your consciousness you will allow permanent healing to take place because healing really is enlightenment—seeing greater light, being more aware. You may notice a few days or a few weeks after having this type of healing that suddenly something may appear a little clearer to you. Or if one were to be asking for some type of special benefit one may observe that some type of understanding is brought about to bring one into a better position to embrace what one is seeking, or it will bring better understanding. It will bring greater awareness; it will bring more light to the illusion that would be presently existing.

Question: 'Can you share with us, ALL THAT IS, what sound affects which chakra. Is it a special sound for a special chakra?'

It is not important as to what chakra is being adjusted by the sound for the chakras are working with each other. When one is not functioning well it affects others, as well as, you may look at them in pairs (Crown/Root; Ajna/Sacral, etc.). If the pair is not working in harmony then there is a bit of an imbalance. So to say that one sound affects just one chakra will not be correct. Sounds would affect different ones depending on each person's ability, or inability, to deal with the circumstances in one's existence.

Question: 'If one were to use an instrument like a Tibetan Bowl during healing, could it be used over the whole body or would the sound have to be directed to one chakra? Couldn't the same sound and the same instrument be used for the whole body?'

Absolutely. You may notice that the sound may change depending upon the vibrational energy coming from the Spirit Being.

Comment: 'So the sound could be telling us where there is an area that needs more work?'

That's right. Yes. Yes. And as you are guided you may work in one area more so than in another area to allow the energy to flow, or to allow the energy to break up, or to allow more of an opening so that greater understanding will flow in. It is important to understand that everything is consciousness, and that everything is based on consciousness. Therefore, we are dealing with enhancing the consciousness.

Quite often when My Spirit Beings meditate or pray or expose themselves to this type of healing they very often have visions. Visions are symbols and for each it is different. There may be some universal symbols that many may understand and yet there will be symbols that will have absolutely no meaning for some and great meaning for others. It is important to try to go within and understand what those symbols mean to you, the individual; to you, the Spirit Being. So you must ask of your Higher Selves or ask of ALL THAT IS, *'What is the meaning of this?' 'What does this mean to me?'* And YOU try to understand what that means to you.

If you are not associated with a symbol, it may mean that you are to research and get to understand more about that symbol. If you understand and have been exposed to that symbol then it is bringing to you the meaning that you have understood from knowing about that symbol. Symbols are for our education. They are tools to help you along your journey. Sometimes you may see a symbol and you may not put any significance to it, and it may not carry any great significance. But if it feels significant to you then seek to understand the greater meaning because it is for you a lesson or a message or an educational process.

Question: 'The Keys of Enoch and the Tree of Life and the Kabbalah have a tremendous amount of symbols. Are they meant for a specific group of people or should all Spirit Beings study them?'

Just like religions; there are many religions for many different types of Spirit Beings. If any of those feel comfortable to you and you would like to embrace it, then by all means embrace it, because it is knowledge of a higher truth. But if it is not flowing very well for you, then I would suggest maybe you need to move in another direction. It is not for every one to embrace each theory.

And I thank you once again for being here to share in the Word. May your days ahead be filled with Peace, and Love, and Joy. May you remember the Truth of Who you really are.

And It Is So. And It Is So. And It Is So.

CHAPTER 17
UNDERSTAND YOUR INTENTIONS

I would like to share with you this evening a reminder that you have chosen to come back here in this earthly environment to advance Spiritually. How are you going to advance spiritually? You must meet challenges. You must conquer these challenges in order to bring you to a greater level of understanding. By conquering these challenges, by getting to a higher level of understanding you will be embracing a higher truth, and that is what spiritual growth is all about, embracing a higher truth.

There are many truths. Some truths are of greater and grander importance than others, just as some of My messengers have come here to Earth with messages, but some have greater or more significant messages than others. Yet all messages are important. But since My Spirit Beings have developed and are at different levels of Spiritual understanding they must continue to grow to develop beyond where they were before.

You will find truths, you will find grander truths, and you will find even grander truths. It is a process that one must accept, one step leading to another. If you were to get to the top of the pyramid, how will you get there?...One step at a time. Or symbolically, allowing your self to be enlightened. Allowing your self to be moving towards a higher truth; allowing your selves to go beyond the limitations that you would have started with. It is a process.

You have chosen virtues to perfect each lifetime that you have returned to Earth. There may be occasions when these virtues may not have been perfected, but you are given other opportunities to continue to seek perfection, because perfection is an ongoing process. You cannot BE perfect; you can only work at BEING perfect.

Some of My Spirit Beings become quite depressed. Some of My Spirit Beings become quite hopeless. Some of My Spirit Beings seek escape from the truth. But the truth is, there is no perfection. There is only the process of perfection. And as long as one continues to work towards advancement one will be advancing, some at a greater speed than others, some at a lesser speed than others, but you must advance if that is what you are choosing to do. If that is your intention, that is what you will be developing. But if it is not your intention, you may be developing spiritually without really knowing or understanding, because your intention has not been solidified.

What is intention? Intention is the thought, the root thought, the thought that goes before the process, the thought that goes before the process. And even intentions can be worked on through a process, for you may observe that your intentions were not clear before the process, or that you did not observe your intentions before the process, or that you did not identify your intentions before the process. But when the intentions have been identified, you can work at bringing them before the process to magnify the process.

Observe your intentions and pay particular attention to your intentions. Intentions are at the root of all actions. There must be a thought before you can get to an action. There must be a thought before you can get to a word. Observe the intentions behind the process. Seek to understand your intentions, seek to make your intentions clear to the Universe, and the Universe will respond in kind, because the Universe operates under the Laws of the Universe. The Laws are for one and the Laws are for all.

I thank you all once again for being here to share your energy with others, to assist not only you but others to be healed, to assist your planet to be healed, to assist your Universe to be healed. I thank you for seeking healing for ALL. And It Is So. And It Is So. And It Is So.

May your days ahead be filled with Peace and Light and Love. May you remember to understand the intentions behind the process. May your intentions be based on Love because Love expands; Love grows; Love encompasses ALL.

And It Is So. And It Is So. And It Is So.

June 16, 1999.

CHAPTER 18
UNDERSTAND THE DIVINE ASPECTS
OF SELF

I thank you very much indeed for being here yet another week to share your devotion with others and to allow your self and others to move towards a higher vibrational energy, and that is to move closer to the Source of the Light.

I have explained in the past that you are a Spark of Light. The Source is Light. You have come from Light; you return to Light. I am sharing in many different ways the most effective manner in which My Spirit Beings can return and claim their fullest Glory. And how can you claim this Glory, or this fullest Glory that is rightfully yours? How can you claim your Spiritual Inheritance?...By continually moving towards the Light. By continually moving towards the Light.

Now this is not something that all of My Spirit Beings can understand, but it is something that I know you will understand if you allow your selves to understand. If you would take the time to spend quietly connecting with your more Divine nature you will begin to understand the nature of the more Divine. If you do not spend time with your computers you will not readily grasp all that you may grasp about computers, and the same applies to your more Divine aspects of Self. If you do not spend the time with the more Divine aspects of Self you will not get to understand the more Divine aspects of Self. Which comes first?

You are first and foremost a Spirit Being. You are a Divine Being and you are here on Earth to remember your spiritual existence. You are here on Earth to remember your Divine nature. You are here on Earth to continue to grow spiritually. They are one and the same, just described by different words, just as My Spirit Beings choose to call Me by different names. Each and every one of you can describe each situation through the use of different words. Does it change the situation? The situation IS what it is. But you can choose to see it for the Beauty that it holds, which will be the more Divine way of seeing your situations and circumstances, or you can choose to see it in the non-Divine ways, which is through blame and guilt and everything derogatory.

Your Divine nature says that **all things are beautiful** and **there is beauty in all situations and in all circumstances.** And as you choose to see the beauty in all situations and all circumstances you assist your selves in connecting with even the more Divine aspects of who you are. Therefore, you allow your selves to see even more beauty in all situations and circumstances. As you continue to dwell in the non-beauty, or in the non-loving aspects of things, you continue to separate your selves from the more Divine. If it is your nature is that of the Divine and you continue to seek the non-Divine, then you are seeking to separate your selves from who you really are. This cannot bring Peace and Joy and Harmony, because you are operating out of harmony, without harmony, therefore, you will be without harmony.

Bless each situation that has been created around you. See the beauty of the experience that it will bring to you and you will be seeking the Divine. The more you can seek the Divine the more you will become the Divine. Your existence here on Earth is rather simple, but the process seems to be difficult for some of My Spirit Beings. There are many different ways of sharing this information but it is important to remember the levels of truth that exist, and not all Spirit Beings are in possession of the higher levels of truth.

Seek to embrace the highest level of truth that you can be comfortable with. Seek understanding in knowing what might be the higher levels of truth. Seek to embrace even what you do not understand rather than denounce what you do not understand. Choose what you are seeking to choose with Peace, with Love, and allow others to choose as well what they are seeking to choose in their own manner.

As you can choose with Peace, you can share Peace, for Peace is an energy that will be extended beyond self; just as non-peace is an energy that extends beyond self, as well. But Peace, being an energy that has greater Light, extends even farther than non-peace. See the beauty of your surroundings. See the beauty of your circumstances. See the beauty of your situations.

I thank you very much indeed again for being here to assist others in knowing Peace, for as you become One with Peace you share Peace with others. Thank you for seeking to know greater Peace.

And It Is So. And It Is So. And It Is So.

June 19, 1999.

CHAPTER 19
ONE WITH THE UNIVERSE

My thanks I give to you once again for being here to listen to some more truths—and as difficult as it may seem, the Word is the Truth and the Truth is the Word. As I have said in the past, there are various layers of Truth just as there are various layers of skin. Not because you are only able to see one layer of skin it means that there are no other layers, and the same applies to the Truth in its many layers.

Not because you are not able to touch it or feel it, or grasp its meaning or understanding, or as I would like you to refer to it, not because you cannot **remember** it, means that it does not exist. Not because you are only able to remember certain truths it means that the other layers of Truth are not present as well.

You breathe and yet if you were to be asked to hold on to what you breathe it will be quite difficult to do so. But what are you breathing? You must be breathing something, otherwise why breathe? Why go through the motions of breathing? Why allow self to experience breathing?

Not only do you as humans breathe but all living things must breathe and they breathe in different ways, yet one just breathes. But there is a more effective way to breathe to get greater benefit from the breathing exercise or to get greater benefit from the breathing truth. So one may breathe unconsciously, or one may choose consciously to breathe.

One may continue to experience one's self in this vast Universe or one may consciously experience one's self in this vast Universe. For you exist and you breathe whether you do it consciously or unconsciously; whether you do it knowingly or unknowingly. But choosing to do it knowingly will allow you to tap into the greater Truths that exist for you, the greater Truths that exist for all of mankind and for all of the Universe. One may choose to eat, or one may choose conscious eating.

The choosing of bringing in greater consciousness into your existence, or into your experience, or into your circumstances, or into your reality, will allow greater Truths to come to the surface, or to penetrate, or to be realized.

There are many layers of consciousness that exist in the Universe and, therefore, that exist within you, for you are One with the Universe and whatever is in the Universe is also within you. What layer of consciousness are you choosing to experience your experiences?

From what floor of this vast building that you call the human experience are you choosing to center your self?...For there are many rooms, and many floors for you to experience your selves here in this earthly plane. You can choose to stay on the ground floor and only see what is directly in front of you, or you can choose to ascend to a higher level and see what is all around.

When you are on the lower levels you can only see what the lower levels are showing you, what is in sight through the lower levels. But as you seek to move up, as you seek to increase your awareness, as you seek to learn greater truths, you can see the vast expansiveness of your reality, if one may call it reality, but we will not get into that subject tonight.

You have been given free will for this journey here on Earth. You may choose to remain attached to the earth-bound way of thinking or you can choose to go to the mountain and seek the greater Truth. It is your free will, for you are loved whether you go to the mountain or whether you stay in the valleys. But because I love ALL of My Spirit Beings equally, I SHARE with them in many, many, different ways how they may remember the grandest Truths, how they can bring Peace and Love and Joy into their Earthly existence.

But it all comes back to you, for it's up to you to exercise your free will in whatever form you choose and in whatever manner you choose; and to experience this earthly realm in whatever manner you choose. But choices bring with it rewards. And as there are various levels of understanding, and experiences, and truths, there are also various levels of rewards. Your choosing will determine the rewards that you will receive. YOUR CHOOSING WILL DETERMINE THE REWARDS YOU WILL RECEIVE. And that is My lesson to you tonight. And It Is So. And It Is So. And It Is So.

I thank you again for being here to share with others and to be healed, for the healing that is shared today is shared with ALL, for we are all part of the WHOLE.

May your days ahead be filled with Peace. May you come to know Peace. May you recognize that you are One with the Light. May you come to know your Self to be One with the Light.

And It Is So. And It Is So. And It Is So.

CHAPTER 20
ABILITY TO RECEIVE

I thank you once again for being here and for seeking to be healed, for whatever you seek you shall receive. The act of seeking allows you to receive if you would receive. Quite often My Spirit Beings are praying, asking, thanking, but when the very things that they are seeking are being given to them they are not able to receive. Therefore, I would like to remind you that part of your praying would be to allow you to also receive and accept ALL that God is trying to share with you. That is a very important prayer.

Although you believe that you are receptive to whatever the Universe or God or your Angels or your Guides are sharing with you, I will have you know that in many, many, many, many, many ways you are NOT accepting, you are NOT receiving the gifts that are being prepared for you. By asking, or by affirming that you are willing to receive and to accept the gifts you will open the doors, so to speak; you will open self, you will open mind to accepting, or you will become aware of how you have been closing the doors and why you have not been receiving even faster than you are receiving.

You are the Controller of the Mind. You must control the thoughts to get you where you would like to be and who you would like to become. And through diligence, through faith, and through trusting, you will get to wherever you are seeking to be or to become. The Universe was created for one and for all. The Universal Laws do not change. You, through controlling the Mind, must change. Each and every one of you is responsible for your personal wellbeing.

God has given you all the tools. And yes, I do understand that your religions have caused you to believe that you are less than who you are; that your religions have not taught you to think of yourselves as powerful; to think of yourselves as the God within. **But I am sharing with you personally tonight that you are the Christ within**. If it is to be it must come through you. Yes, you ask for assistance, you ask to be helped, you ask to be guided, you ask for divine energy to flow through you, you ask for Angels to be with you, but **YOU...must... be...the...driving...force...behind...ANY...changes... that you are seeking to bring into your existence.**

You can not be healed by thanking God for healing and not expect that YOU are responsible for maintaining that healing. One can be healed just as fast as one can become separated from God, and one can become separated from God just as fast as one can be healed. Your thoughts must be used in the appropriate manner to bring you into Oneness with the Christ within, your first step to mastering self. I will allow you to continue and we will share any questions as time permits.

I would like Angela to share with you now some information I gave her recently. Yet another tool to assist you in moving forward in reclaiming your Oneness, in remembering WHO you truly are.

As received from ALL THAT IS:

"Let each day be a new day to renew your thoughts, to renew your beliefs, and to bring you closer to knowing purity of mind.

Each day take just ONE aspect of an EGO belief, examine it, understand where and how it originated; see the illusion of its existence, and choose to embrace a grander Truth. Speak this grander truth to the ego no less than three times whenever it reminds you of the illusion. And continue to affirm the Truth until the ego understands the new belief, which is, until you choose to experience the new belief.

Only through your diligence, your desire, will the ego release the old for the new, the illusion for the Truth, as you may understand it at the time. And It Is So."

You are the change creator—no one but you will bring about changes to your ego. Pray that you will use the Strength and the Power and the Love of the Father or of the Christ Self that is within you to assist you in making the changes to your ego-belief system.

Use affirmations to assist the ego in remembering the Truth. It is important also to affirm who you are seeking to become, not who you believe your self to be at the present time. **Remember that the mind has no concept of time and can not distinguish future from present.** Say it as you are seeking it to BE-COME and it (mind) shall remember that it IS.

You are the Creator of your dreams, your visions, your reality. God provides you with the tools, the abilities, the gifts to allow you to be-come WHO you are seeking to BECOME. Use your abilities, the tools, the gifts to become WHO you are seeking to become. And It Is So. And It Is So. And It Is So.

Comment: 'We need to get to the cellular level, not by just changing our perception.'

Every thought is at the cellular level. By changing your thoughts you are changing the cells. You can strengthen the body just as you strengthen the mind. Whatever you put in, is what would affect what is within. Whatever you put into your mind affects the mind. Whatever you put into your body affects the body. But **thought** is the creator of what ever you put into your mind or whatever you put into your body **because nothing happens without thought.**

So thought is the generator of everything. Therefore, you must change thought, even while changing or while adding to the physical structure of the cells. But the memory, what you are doing by enhancing the quality of the intake of food, is that you are strengthening the cells. But thought must be changed.

So even though one strengthens the cells and allows the body to feel rejuvenated, in order to overcome illness one must change the cellular structure by changing the thought, because the cells are going to renew themselves, and what is renewed is what IS. Therefore, if what IS is not perfection, what is going to be renewed will be non-perfection, even though you can see the perfection in it.

How many times have we said that this food is not good for me, or that is not good for me. When our thought is that a food is bad for the body then it will not be good for the body.

Comment: 'So now I can say coffee is good for me!' (Laughter)

That's right. 'But I choose. I choose not to drink it.'...And it is good for you! These are the things you have to put into the mind. And by changing the mind you change your cells because the mind is within those cells. The mind is everywhere and cells are everywhere. If you've got a pain in the ankle, it is something in the mind that is causing this pain, therefore, you must get in touch with what is causing the pain, and you will understand what is in the mind.

In order for one to be truly healthy one must only entertain healthy thoughts. You do not embrace anything that is not good, or not worthy, or not honest, and therefore you put nothing that is not good, not worthy, or not honest within you and you will become healthy. But if you think in thoughts of, 'This is not good. I am ill. I am sick. I am tired. I am weary. I cannot do this. I am unable to do that.'—Or thoughts of any types of fear, you create separation. And how can separation be shown to you? In subtle ways at first, but eventually it must be manifested through the physical, it must be manifested through the physical.

And just as your thoughts have caused the separation, your thoughts can heal the separation by:

Thinking thoughts of Oneness,
Repeating thoughts of Oneness,
Living thoughts of Oneness,
Seeing through the eyes of Oneness,
Embracing the Oneness,
Blessing the Oneness,
And you will be come as
One.

You are the change creator. You now choose to either believe what you are being told or to believe in what you believed to be the truth as was shown to you. You, collectively, are responsible for the illusions that have been allowed to continue to be part of your earthly existence because you did not choose to embrace the grander truths. But you now have the opportunity to make those changes, not only for you, but for many others. But that is only a choice.

Again, one must, in the silence, come to understand the benefits of knowing a grander truth. Only through understanding and trusting and having faith in what is being shown to you as the grander truths, will you seek to achieve those grander truths. While the benefits are not meaningful to you there will be less desire to make those changes. But changes can only be made through you, and by you, for you. And that is My lesson tonight. And It Is So. And It Is So. And It Is So.

Question not recorded.

You now have to ask yourselves at all times, *'Is what I believe a Spiritual Truth or is it a man-made truth?' 'Is it an ego trip, or a Spiritual Trip?'* It is your choice. If it is you want to be on a spiritual trip then you must change your way of thinking based on the knowledge that you believed you had, and now really embrace the knowledge, because knowledge can only come from God.

The ego deals with illusions and perceptions. When you are dealing with the conditioned mind, the ego mind, or when you are on an ego trip, you are only dealing with illusions; you are not dealing with Truths. Yet in another sense, each is a truth of the believer, because if you believe something to be so, it is your truth. And if you believe something to be not so, it is still your truth.

Yet there is a greater and grander Truth and that is the Truth of the God Most High or the Universal Truth, however you may choose to think of it. So although those are aspects of truth, in the bigger picture they are really illusions when one compares them to the higher Spiritual Truths. In that context, you seek to eliminate the illusions created by ego and bring into your belief system the Truths as shown to you through the God Mind.

I thank you once again for being here and for sharing this Truth. May your days ahead be filled with Peace, with Light, with Love. May you come to know that you are the Light, that you are the Peace, that you are the Love. And may you share your Light with the World.

And It Is So. And It Is So. And It Is So.

CHAPTER 21
HEAL THE EGO

I thank you for doing your part to bring about healing for your brothers and sisters. I thank you for doing your part to bring about healing for this Universe. I thank you for doing your part to share healing with others around you. The greatest gift that you can give to humanity is the gift of healing. As you heal, humanity heals. As you remain attached to the ego, humanity remains attached to the ego. For every one that heals, thousands are healed. Thank you for assisting thousands to become whole.

It is quite a challenge indeed to overcome the ego. And all healing is about the ego. There is nothing else to heal. Since all healing is to repair separation, the only aspect that becomes separated is the aspect of mind that abides by man-made beliefs. As you continue to heal the ego you become as Truth. When you embrace Truth, you are at one with Truth. When you are at one with Truth, you will no longer choose to embrace man-made beliefs, for one can not KNOW the Truth and believe the illusions. When one knows the Truth, one remains in the Truth. Truth, unlike perception, does not change. As you become one with Truth you will not change what you know to be Truth.

It is important to remember that the ego was not formed overnight, to use a phrase from your terminology. Therefore, one must not expect that the ego will be erased or healed or become one with the God Self overnight. It is impractical. It is ego thinking. The ego will try to tell you that it is taking too long. The ego may try to tell you that it is not working because you have tried a few methods and yet here again you still don't know the truth. But just as you have created the ego, you have the power to change and bring about the truth.

The ego must be dealt with, at times, very seriously but yet can be dealt with very lovingly. At times one may have to be very stern, and yet at times, one can be very coaxing. Just as you will deal with a child, you will deal with the ego, for the ego really is the child. The ego does not know the truth. Sometimes it is necessary to become quite stern even with your friends, your brothers, your sisters, your children; and sometimes one can bring about changes by being ever so gentle.

But one MUST be observing, patient, and vigilant. It is only through a great desire to change that one changes. Only through a desire to know greater peace, or greater love, or greater freedom, would one make changes. That must be the choice that you must bear. If it is important enough for you to become master of your ego then you will make changes. If ego is serving you to be who you are and who you would like to become then there is no need to make changes. You must choose.

You have been given free choice. No one is dictating that you must change. The choice is yours. Choose to become One with God, choose to be the miracle maker, choose to know Peace, choose to BE Love, choose to become whole, or choose to remain who you are. And that is My lesson to you tonight. And It Is So. And It Is So. And It Is So.

Are there any questions on this ever important ego, yet not so important?

Question not recorded.

Yes, the ego is an obstacle. Once you overcome the ego you become One with God, you become One with ALL THAT IS, you become One with the Father, you become One with the Christ Self, you become as the Higher Spiritual aspects of who you are. The ego hinders you, the ego prevents you, the ego holds you back, because the ego is not based on truth. **And no, the ego was not created to assist you in becoming whole. The ego has been created by man because of the separation.**

When you chose to know your self to be independent through this journey here on Earth you gave up all memory of spiritual truths. Therefore you have, over the centuries, replaced spiritual truths with man-made beliefs. The ego has been created by those man-made truths. But one can overcome the ego; one must search for the Truth. And it is important to replace one thing with another. If you are replacing the ego, then you must replace the ego with the Truth. You must replace an ego belief with a Spiritual Truth. If you are editing a tape, and you just clear the tape and do not replace it with anything, there will be nothing.

Question not recorded.

I choose not to make predictions. There was a time when humanity was very much evolved and therefore did not have to survive by these creations of the lower self. And we are returning to a more evolved state with the healings that are being shared. And the more we can heal the ego; the more we can get back to the spiritual truths, the faster humanity can become evolved.

I thank you once again for being here and for sharing in the Word. May your days ahead be filled with Peace, with Love, with Light. May you come to know the Joy that is rightfully yours. May you be One with Love. May you be One with ALL THAT IS. May you remember that you are Spirit having a human experience and that all of God's creations are Spirit having earthly experiences, as you are experiencing your self as a human here on Earth.

And It Is So. And It Is So. And It Is So.

CHAPTER 22
BE EXPOSED TO THE TRUTH

I wish to thank you all for being here and to once again move forward with your healing. As I have said in the past, for every one who becomes healed thousands will become healed. I thank you for endeavoring to be healed.

We have been talking lately about the ego and I will continue on that topic today. The mind is broken up into many different aspects. Some of My Spirit Beings call it one thing, some of them call it another. Just as I am called by many different names, so too, the ego mind is known by many different labels. Regardless of how one may choose to call the ego, the ego represents that aspect of mind that adheres to earthly thinking. The ego abides by earthly laws and when I refer to earthly laws I refer to man-made laws.

And yes, you must abide by earthly laws which are state laws, or which are country laws; laws that provide for your welfare based on state principles or on governmental principles. If you are in Rome you must abide by the Roman Laws. If you are in Canada you must abide by the Canadian Laws; or by the laws of your region, or province, or community.

But these are not the laws of man that I am referring to. I am referring to the beliefs of mankind that have not been established as state laws, for the want of a better terminology. I am referring to the beliefs of mankind over the years that dictate how one must think, how one must behave, even outside of the laws established by those in power. The ego is that part of the mind that believes in what it chooses to believe without really knowing the grander Truth.

As it has been written on different occasions the ego can be thought of as the "lower self." One refers to the lower self as opposite to the more Divine aspect of who you are. One refers to the lower self as that aspect of mankind that is attached to senses, that is attached to emotions, that is attached to things of a physical nature, rather than that aspect of Self that knows greater peace because of its communication with the Divine.

In order for one to understand the difference, one must understand what the Divine nature is like so that one may know the opposite of the Divine. If one does not make oneself aware of what is Truth, of what falls into the Laws of the Divine, one will not be able to understand when one is operating out of the Laws of the Divine. In other words, if you do not know what consists of Divine thoughts, or of Divine beliefs, or of Divine ways, one will not recognize when one is thinking in other than Divine ways, that one is thinking in non-Divine ways. To correct one aspect one must know what the opposite is. To make changes one must know something different to change to.

It is very easy for some of us to criticize another and to say, 'Why are you not doing such, and such, and such?' But if we are not exposed to something different we will not know how to react or to behave to such, and such, and such. If we have only exposed our selves to one way of thinking and one way of behaving then there is nothing in our frame-of-reference to allow us to know something different.

Therefore, in order to change from ego thinking one must make oneself knowledgeable or aware of Divine thinking. One must understand what is considered mastery over the lower senses.

Only through exposure to something different can one change from that which we believe we know to that which is the Truth. We must first be exposed to the Truth. We must become aware of the Truth in order to embrace the Truth. Without knowing, and in this context I am using it as being exposed to, rather than spiritually knowing the Truth, one will not know the reason why one must change to the Truth in order to work towards the Truth.

One must know there is something different in order to work at something different. One must believe that there is something better in order to work at seeking what is better. Without bringing your selves into awareness of the "better" or the more peaceful, the more divine, one will not know what one is striving to achieve. One must expose one's self to more Divine ways of thinking so that one may seek to achieve the more Divine ways to thinking. It is only by becoming exposed to something can one strive to attain that something. And that is My lesson to you tonight. And It Is So. And It Is So. And It Is So.

One can not achieve what one has no awareness about, that one has no knowledge of, that one has no exposure to. If you expose yourselves to earth-bound thinking you will not know anything different than earth-bound thinking. Consider for a moment not learning about the ways and means of those of another country. If you do not understand how they think, how they behave, and what their rules are for that particular country, you will never be able to understand anyone from that country. You may never even realize that there are other countries out there. But by taking the time to investigate and learn about those of other countries you can now choose to understand and even embrace those of other countries, should you choose to go to those countries.

May this explanation help you to seek knowledge of the more Divine so that you may choose to become part of the more Divine; that you may know freedom from the bondage of your earthly attachments; that you may know freedom from the bondage of the flesh; that you may know freedom from the bondage of your emotions. And It Is So. And It Is So. And It Is So.

My thanks to you again. May your days ahead be filled with Peace, with Light, and with Love. May you become One with Love.

And It Is So. And It Is So. And It Is So.

CHAPTER 23
YOU ARE DIVINITY

I would like to thank each of you for being here to share in the healing of your World. I would like to take you through a meditation this evening to assist you in identifying more with who you really are.

> Try to see your self as a bird. Know that you are a holy bird because you see your selves through the eyes of holiness. As a bird, where are you seeking to go? Spend a few minutes being the bird. Now, you are choosing to bring a message to someone. What is that message?...When you are ready open your eyes.

This is a form of meditation that will allow you to understand the freedom of who you really are with the limitations that you are setting for your self, or that you could set for yourself. As you begin to observe all around the meditation process it tells you more about you. Try this on your own, in your quiet time, and you will be given many insights into the self.

I would like to answer your questions this evening and I know you have another part to complete as well.

Question: 'What does it mean by "Spirit lives" as received in meditation? Is it that ALL THAT IS Spirit lives within each of us?'

Yes. But what it also means is that there is no death to Spirit. Spirit is Eternal. The body is NOT who you are. This body, after it has fulfilled its role, is no longer needed, just as a wedding dress—since we are all of female energy here in female energy form and can therefore associate with this. The wedding dress is of little use after the wedding; so too is the body of little use after the resurrection, and that is the physical resurrection that I am speaking of, and not the spiritual resurrection, for one can have both.

Question: 'While doing meditation I seem to be able to get to a certain point and not be able to get beyond that point. Is it some limitation of my own, or is it that I am not ready to go further?'

Yes to both. Which one comes first, however?...The limitation that you have set for your self, or the inability to move on? We now know as Spirit, if we are not held down by our earthly beliefs, that we can become all that we can become. Therefore, you must give your self permission to progress beyond where you are right now and know that as Spirit you are Divinity, and Divinity is Spirit and lives on. Therefore you can become and be and go Eternally.

Question: 'When we hear things in other languages that we do not speak, will we still understand the message?'

Yes. The conscious mind, not understanding will not readily connect, but at a deeper level you are understanding, because the mind is the Mind of God and, therefore, the God aspect of the mind understands and knows everything. It is, however, advisable that if one were to really conquer, or to share in progressing, one should really connect with what one is hearing or knowing.

Question: 'I was wondering about the mantras since they are not in our language but in another language.'

The messages are being internalized and by repeating them you are sending out to the Universe the significance of the words. But it's a very good question, because one can do basically the same thing in one's own language and therefore fully connect with what one is doing. But the message is still sent out. The God Self understands what you are saying. The God Self knows that the intention is there and the Universe receives what is being sent out, because the Universe understands all. It is a way to go beyond the conscious mind and to quiet the conscious mind and yet, why not give thanks in a language that is understood by you? But it's a choice.

Mantras are very powerful tools and help one in going beyond the surface, just as mandalas are very powerful tools that one cannot easily recognize. But yet it is recognized by the God mind and, again, a way to move beyond the conscious thinking, move beyond the ego thinking. Ego might say, *'I can't understand anything.'* Or, *'What does this mean? It just looks like a lot of lines and drawings. What is the significance of it?'*...Whereas it goes below the surface.

Question not recorded.

I would say you are going about it the right way. You are sharing beautifully with the children of the world since there was much mention of helping children. You also start with a prayer asking for guidance, asking for your Angels and your Guides to be with you, and that is all that you actually need. As you call on your God and your Angels and your Guides to allow you to understand, you will tap into greater understanding and one cannot ask for any more.

It is necessary to observe as you go along though the opportunities that the ego will take to pull you away from keeping focused on your true purpose, and My recommendation would be to observe self and observe the group, because you are in a group to help each other. So observe what is going on and try to keep the group focused and not allow "ego" to get the upper hand. As I recommended in the past, closing off with a prayer, or as you do, is of great benefit. My only suggestion for this would be to just observe how the ego can infiltrate and cause you to lose focus.

My thanks I give to you again for being here and for sharing in this time of healing. May your days ahead be filled with Peace, with Light, with Love. May you remember that you are truly Spirit and that you are here on Earth to share your healing with others. You are here to be healed, to remember WHO you truly are. May the healing that has begun today continue to bring you into Oneness.

And It Is So. And It Is So. And It Is So.

CHAPTER 24
VISUALIZE YOURSELVES AS DIVINITY

I thank you all very much for being here this evening to continue your healing, not only for you but for your planet and for the world. Healing is a process. It is a process of taking you back to your Divinity. As Spirit Beings being away from your home, you have lost contact with who you really are. You have chosen the veil of forgetfulness so that you may once again grow into the Divine aspect of self that you knew before coming to this earthly plane.

I would like you to think in terms of you being a Divine Spirit Being playing the role in this human body. **If you can visualize your selves as DIVINITY you can more readily return to Divinity**. The difficulty in returning to divinity lies in the separation. You have become so separated from who you really are that you have begun to believe in the separated self. **One must look at this separated self as an ACT**, as part of a play that will allow you to progress, that will allow you to become, that will allow you to perfect, that will allow you to overcome, that will allow you to attain your chosen path.

If you see your selves as human it is difficult to grasp being anything other than human. When you can view your self as an Angel, per se, choosing to come to Earth to remember that you are an Angel, it would be much easier to attain your Angelic status.

YOU ARE SPIRIT. You have chosen this existence and you have chosen it for very, very, very, very good and profound reasons. You are an expression of God. You are God in whatever you are choosing to be. You are representing God. You are God's messengers. And if you are God's messengers then each and every one becomes a messenger for God.

When humanity can recognize the Divinity that lies beneath the human form, humanity will know Peace on Earth. Until Peace on Earth is a way of life, God's expressions will be less than whole. You are here with each other to assist each other. You are mirrors to each other. If My Angels do not play the role of the thoughts of man, man will not be able to observe his thoughts. If My Angels do not play the roles based on the vibration of man's thoughts, man will not understand man's thinking.

This may be a difficult concept for many to grasp but for those of you who are able at this time to understand that concept, become as the Light to lead others in greater understanding. The more of My Spirit Beings who can observe themselves in others and assist in allowing others to understand this greater truth, to them is the Power to Heal the World; **for there is no greater power than the power to see oneself in ALL the expressions of God.**

And if there are any questions I will be more than happy to take the time to share with you, if not tonight at some other time, for you may need to think on these things to allow the significance to take hold.

My thanks I give to you again for the healing that you are bringing to this world by the healing that you are bringing to you. And It Is So. And It Is So. And It Is So.

The following are responses to questions not verbalized.

When you heal the separation the body will become healed, if the body has not deteriorated to the point of non-healing.

First of all, the body is only showing you that the Spirit within is feeling the separation based on the human's point of view. In other words, if we can use the terms that you are familiar with now—Spirit is feeling separated because of the ego. Because of your earth-bound thinking, Spirit feels separated, or ego is separating you from your spiritual connection, therefore it is manifesting, it is showing you that there is a separation through the effects of the body.

And yet one may come to Earth with less than a perfect body in the eyes of man, so it is very difficult for most to understand this concept. When one returns to wholeness, this means to return to the wholeness that has been designed for you, for the Spirit Being that you are, not necessarily what collective man has decided is the norm.

***

You do not have different spirits, you are One Spirit. Your Spirit is eternal....One Soul. Your Soul is eternal. And your Soul is choosing a body that is going to know certain defects (as man will call it)....It could be ailments, in order for you to grow spiritually. In other words, a Spirit may assume the home into a body that will be, what you may call, autistic.

Why would a Spirit choose to have a body that is going to be autistic, one may ask?...Because that would be the greatest avenue for spiritual healing for that Spirit. That is the avenue that will bring about the greatest form of healing for that Spirit. Maybe that Spirit needs to know complete surrender, and how else will one choose complete surrender other than being in a form that one has no control over? And I am speaking in terms of varying degrees, and I am using that as an example.

One may choose to be in a body that seems to be less than whole, and we will take for instance a child that may be in a body that has developed heart conditions. But that Spirit Being has chosen to be in that body, not only to bring about greater healing to its own Spirit, but to assist in the healing of those who will be connected to that Spirit in this lifetime or in the current lifetime.

***

Whatever you have not been able to deal with effectively, what you have not been able to conquer, will be what you bring back again, or carry forward, or retain in different forms until you can get back to the point of knowing Divinity; until you can get back to the point of knowing your selves to be pure Love. Just as you use different vehicles to get you to where you are choosing to be, you are using different methods to allow you to become whole.

So what is the best method? Pray for that friend, send Light and Love to that friend and acknowledge that that friend is an expression of Divinity choosing whatever they are choosing for their own and highest good. It is up to them if they overcome or not overcome. It is their path. Each and every one must be allowed to travel the path as they choose.

***

Everything is a messenger. Everything is a mirror— EVERYTHING. If you can look at each other and look at things around you and just seek to know what is the message, you will be sharing much love with the soul, because everything in your path is a message to bring you into greater awareness of Who you are seeking to become. Everything in your path is a message to assist you in becoming who you have chosen to become.

> **Seek the messages that are around you. Seek to observe what is being shown to you. Seek to know the YOU within, for that is what this life is all about, getting to know the YOU within, getting in touch with the God within, getting in touch with the Messenger within.**

***

When we can see ourselves in terms of **universal** we have moved from the realm of personal and we are doing a bigger and larger job. Again, bearing in mind that all work is God's work, it is just of a different nature.

***

Unconditional Love is the highest form of Love.
Unconditional Love is reuniting you to the God within.
You can not become reunited with God
Without Unconditional Love.
God IS Unconditional Love.
When you can know Unconditional Love
You can be come as God.

How can you know that you are Unconditional Love without having opportunities to express unconditional love— to express it, to know it, to feel it, to be it?

***

Illness is caused by an accumulation of negative cells or negative energy, which in turn has caused your energy centers to become reversed or blocked. When your Chi, or Ki, or

Divine Energy cannot get into those areas that are affected, the areas become more dis-eased and, therefore, continue to dis-engage themselves from the normal processes. When healing takes place, the centers become opened. But unless one pays attention to **self** and abides by the messages given through others, deterioration will continue and one may return to the original state of un-wellness. However, when one has a genuine desire to become healed, the desire is answered and healing will continue.

> Remember
> Whatever is in the mind
> Is also in the Universe
> For there is no separation
> Except in the mind.

The illusion is believing that each is separate. The TRUTH is that you are each connected. Not only connected to each other, but that you are connected to ME. When one breaks through the illusion and accepts the TRUTH, rejoicing takes place and PEACE will reign. Greater Peace brings greater Joy. Greater Joy grows into ECSTASY. That is truly Peace on Earth.

***

There are many ways of healing. Quite often we become attached to certain ways of healing and believe that if we do not do this, or we do not do that, we are not being healed; but healing takes place on many levels and in many different ways. You have received quite a healing here tonight although you may not have done your chanting, as Angela insists that you do. But please know and believe and accept that you did receive a healing and healing did take place. Believe it, accept it, and it will be so.

***

May your days ahead be filled with Peace, with Light, with Love. May you remember that you are My Angels, that you are My Messengers, that you are all My Children, you are all ONE. Thank you once again for being here and for assisting in the healing of others.

And It Is So. And It Is So. And It Is So.

CHAPTER 25
ONLY LOVE CAN BRING YOU PEACE

I give thanks to you for being here to participate in this period of healing. The healing of one is the healing of many. The healing of many is the healing of many, many more, for as you are healed so will many others heal. For you will become as the Light that will light the darkness for others to see.

You have been made in the Image and Likeness of God, therefore, you have been given all of the gifts and abilities of God. In order for those gifts and abilities to be made manifest one must continue to, metaphorically, open the doors so that healing will take place, and healing means the return to wholeness. In other words, remembering that you are whole. And that is what healing does: removes the truth of man to allow the Truth of God to penetrate and to be made active in your earthly existence.

Healing then is symbolic of change, for as healing takes place changes take place, changes that you may not be aware of at the time, for there are many subtle energies within and about you that you are not conscious of or about.

Healing causes a new thought to penetrate;
A God-thought, if you would look at it like that, to
penetrate
And become mingled with your present thinking.

And the more healing that takes place the more God thoughts are brought into your existence, therefore, the more God-thinking is made manifest in your lives, per se.

And there are many forms of healing as there are many forms of religions, as there are many forms of understanding, for there are many expressions of Who I Am. It would be unfair for Me to create only a few types of healing for the multitudes of expressions that exist of ME. There are, however, some forms of healing that are of a higher vibration and, therefore, are more effective, or becomes effective more readily. But all healings take you to the same place—to your God connection to hear the thoughts of God, to know the thoughts of God, to become aware of the thoughts of God, so that these thoughts may be integrated into your earthly existence.

In order for one to know true Peace one must know true Love and true Love, as I have explained in the past, is based on Acceptance. And how can one get to the place of Acceptance?...

THROUGH FORGIVENESS.

I Forgive all that I know and do not know.
I Forgive all that I remember and not remember.
I Forgive all that I understand and do not understand.
I Forgive ALL.

As one continues to forgive, one will begin to know greater Love. It is a Law of the Universe. Even if you do not understand what you are doing, even if you do not understand the reason, by forgiving, and forgiving, and forgiving, you will be moving forward into a higher state of BEING, therefore, you will become as Love. And in order to know Peace one must become as Love, for only Love can bring you Peace. Only Love can bring you Peace. Accept that you do not know, that you do not understand, but FORGIVE and you will, therefore, be loving and accepting what you do not know and what you do not understand. And this is yet another way to have Peace on Earth as it is in Heaven. And that is My lesson to you tonight. And It Is So. And It Is So. And It Is So.

I thank you once again for being here. May your days ahead be filled with Peace, with Light, and with Love. May you come to know the Peace, the Light, and the Love that is yours. May you remember who you truly are.

And It Is So. And It Is So. And It Is So.

CHAPTER 26
WHAT IS SPOKEN
IS THE FORCE THAT CREATES

I thank you for taking the time to be here to hear the Word and how important the Word truly is. You have been created by the Word and you create by the Word. Every Word that is uttered brings about creation. Every Word that is thought brings about creation. It is My wish for mankind to understand the importance of the words that they share with each other. It is not understood at this time that what is spoken is the force that creates. What is spoken is the force that creates.

It is very important for My Spirit Beings to examine the words that they share in thought as well as what they speak. It is believed that what is said in jest, remains in jest, but that is not how the Universe operates. The Laws have been in place for ALL, and the Universe can not differentiate what is jest for one and what is prayer for another. WORDS are prayers, either thought or spoken. And just as you create by not being aware that you create based on what is spoken, one can become aware and create based on what one chooses by speaking what one wants to create. Create by default, or create through choice.

As one understands the Universal Laws, one must apply these Universal Laws to bring about changes or one will be perpetually stuck in the creation by default. And that is a term that should be readily understood by most at this time since you are in the age of computer knowledge. I cannot simplify the message of "Words" in any other way but to remind, and remind, and remind that creation can be brought about through conscious thinking, conscious speaking; or creation will be brought about through unconscious thinking and speaking.

If you think and say that you can't, then you will not. If you choose to know differently you must think and say differently and it will be brought about as you think and say. It is a Law of the Universe. Universal Laws do not change—they are not man-made; they exist for one, they exist for all.

CHOOSE your Words carefully. CHOOSE your Thoughts carefully. They are your creations. And that is My message to you tonight. And It Is So. And It Is So. And It Is So.

My thanks I give to you once more for being here. May your days ahead be filled with Peace, with Light and with Love. May you know that you are the Light; that you are Peace; that you are Love. May you be filled with Peace, and Light and Love.

And It Is So. And It Is So. And It Is So.

CHAPTER 27
CLOSER TO LOVE

And I give thanks to you for allowing Me to be in your home, in your lives, in your thoughts. I thank you for this opportunity to share the Word with as many of those who are willing to receive and accept the Word.

You have all elected to have free choice in all that you think, and say, and do. This journey here on Earth is by free choice. Your journey on Earth is one of free choice. You may choose to continue to live in ignorance of a greater and grander truth of who you truly are, or you may choose to reconnect with the greater and grander truth of who you truly are, all part of your free choice.

For those who are choosing to reconnect with their Souls, or their Spirits, or with their Higher Selves, however you may want to call that aspect of you that is truly the Divine aspect, greater joys will lie ahead. Greater peace will be in store for you, for as you work through the challenges that this earthly existence brings to you, you will be embracing your greater spiritual truths.

Only through life's challenges, only through the challenges that are being shared with you can you get to know a greater you. Without the challenges, without the frustrations, without the pain, there really is no room for growth, for growth can only come by seeking to be other than who you are at any given moment. It is only by the stretching, the turning, the breaking out of what was, that one can become what one is seeking to become. And it is not a becoming that becomes instantaneously, but a becoming that becomes gradually. By every choice that one makes through love one brings one's self closer to love. By every choice that one makes out of fear, one is keeping one's self rooted to fear.

Although on the surface it may seem like the easier or the more peaceful option, growth lies in the **trust** that you can have in the greater power of our God to always take care of us, to always look after us, and to acknowledge who you are based on the love that you are. That is where the greater peace exists. That is where you will come to know that you are truly moving towards a higher attainment of Love, a higher attainment of Godliness, a higher attainment of Truth.

When one seeks to know a greater truth, one abides by and in a greater truth. When one seeks to live a greater truth, one becomes a greater truth. As one continues to grow in truth, one accepts the truth of who you truly are. One accepts the love of who you truly are. One accepts the love and truth of the powers that are buried deep within who you truly are, for all powers lie within. One does not have to wait for them to be given to you. But one must seek to use the powers that are lying dormant within for them to become active, for you are all that you are.

You are the Image and Likeness of God and God is ALL, therefore, you too are ALL. You have within you all that you can ever seek to be. And that is My message to you tonight. And It Is So. And It Is So. And It Is So.

I give thanks to you once again for being here, for hearing the Word, and for abiding by the Word. For it is only through living the Word that one becomes as the Word. **It is through the experiencing that one becomes what one is seeking**

to become. It is through the experiencing of the Word that one becomes the Word. May the Words that you hear become the Words that you experience. May the Words that you hear become the Words that you are.

And It Is So. And It Is So. And It Is So.

CHAPTER 28
ALL KNOWLEDGE AND TRUTH
LIE WITHIN

I give thanks to you once again for being here to hear the Word, to bring healing to others, to know Peace, to become as Love, and to assist in the evolution of this World.

You have indeed taken the veil of forgetfulness, or the veil of separation, when you agreed to return to Earth to assist in this universal healing process. And it seems that the truth is really not the truth, for it is very far removed from the illusions that we have been allowed to experience during our times of remembrance while on this journey.

I would like you once again to think of yourselves as Spirit having a human experience. Accept and believe that you do not remember the Truth; that what you have been exposed to are the illusions based on man's perceptions. Seek to bring about the Truth, to tap into the Truth, for the Truth lies within. **Seek to remember just one aspect of Truth each day and you will be allowed to remember one aspect of Truth each day.** Although the aspect may seem very small, all Truth takes you closer to Who you really are and Where you really belong.

All Knowledge and Truth lie within and it is therefore your responsibility to seek to know what is not now knowledge to you. Seek to become part of Truth, to share Truth, and to BE Truth, and by so doing you bring Truth to this universal network.

I have shared with you in many different ways information to allow you to get to greater and grander Truths. You have all chosen to be here at this time to fulfill a duty, a function, a goal for your evolution and for the evolution of your brothers and sisters of this world. There is never just one technique or one avenue for getting to the Truth. Explore as many as you may be exposed to and choose what is most comfortable for you until you choose again, until you choose again, and again, and again. For choice is the only constant. Through choosing one continues to realign one's self with a Greater and Grander TRUTH. And that is My message to you tonight. And It Is So. And It Is So. And It Is So.

May your days ahead be filled with Peace, with Light, with Love. May you continue to grow in remembrance of Who you truly are. May you continue to seek greater and grander Truths. May you know Who you really are. And It Is So. And It Is So. And It Is So.

My Love I give to you that you may be filled with Love, that you may become as Love, so that you may share the Love and the Light that you are with all others.

And It Is So. And It Is So. And It Is So.

CHAPTER 29
EMBRACE THE TRUTH

A nd I give thanks to you for being here to continue to hear the Word. You have heard time and time again the phrase, "Hear the Word and the Word will set you free." But how many of My Spirit Beings really hear the Word?

I shared with you on a previous occasion that by abiding by the Word you will know freedom from bondage, therefore, hearing is abiding. Hearing, as used in this context, is more than allowing your physical hearing apparatus to do the work, but by going deeper within and allowing your Spiritual apparatus to bring about a greater understanding of what the physical apparatus may have heard.

It is only by embracing the Truth
That one can become as the Truth.
It is only by embracing the
Words of Truth
That one can walk the Truth.
And only when one walks the Truth
Can one really BE an expression of Truth.
Truth, therefore, remains just a theory,
Unless one walks the Truth,
Unless one becomes an expression of Truth,
Unless one lives the Truth.

And it is only by living the Truth can
Freedom from bondage be obtained.
One can not become FREE from the
Illusions that you have been exposed to.
Freedom lies in
Expressing the Truth,
Being the Truth,
And therefore,
Sharing the Truth.

And what does sharing the Truth mean?

Simply BEING the Truth. As you become Truth, you share Truth, for you cannot share what you are not, and you cannot not share what you are. Truth, therefore, is to be shared. It is only through the sharing, which is through the BEING, that you become as TRUTH.

And that is My lesson for you tonight. May the Truth that lies within be expressed so that you may BE the TRUTH. And It Is So. And It Is So. And It Is So.

Thank you for being here and for sharing your time in this manner. May your days ahead be filled with Peace, with Light, with Love. May you remember Who you truly are.

And It Is So. And It Is So. And It Is So.

CHAPTER 30
YOU ARE PERFECTION

My thanks I give to you for being here, for seeking healing not only for you but for many, many others. I thank you very much indeed for the work that you are doing on behalf of your brothers and sisters, not only the brothers and sisters that you are aware of and that you are helping in this present lifetime, to use a phrase that you would understand, but also all of your brothers and sisters who are able to receive and accept what is being shared with them.

This evening I would like to share with you yet another form of meditation, one that will allow you to go within and receive the answers to your questions, the questions that are not being readily understood, the ones that are taking a little bit more time to be understood or to be remembered.

> As in the past, see your self in your garden of beauty, whatever garden you choose to be your garden of beauty. You are choosing to go for a walk in this garden. But you will come to a place of silence, some place that feels very peaceful to you, whether it is a pond...or a river...or in the midst of the trees...or lying in the grass...whatever is most peaceful for you. Now ask a question...Give thanks and continue on your walk...or return....When you are ready open your eyes.

Discussion ensued.

You are indeed discussing a very important subject, the subject of seeing things as they are, instead of seeing the Truth of things.

The more of My Spirit Beings who can see the perfection in every one and in every thing will bring about more perfection in this Universe. The more of My Spirit Beings who will see only perfection in others will bring about perfection in themselves. For if your eyes are on the obstacles, which will be the dis-ease or the dis-comfort, then that is what you will continue to bring about. But if your focus, or your attention, will be placed on the **perfection** of Who you truly are, and I mean each and every one of you, then it will be easier for each and every one to return to that perfection.

If there is no thought sent out about perfection it is rather difficult for perfection to be realized. But when one starts to recognize perfection then perfection is all there is. Perfection will be all that you see. Perfection will be all that will be brought into existence. Perfection is symbolic of Love.

If one understands the Truth of Love one realizes that it is Perfection. For when one can forgive and accept, one truly loves. By forgiving and accepting one just IS. When one just IS, one is LOVE, for that is Who you are. You are Love. You are Perfection. You are Spirit.

If we send out thoughts of perfection to each other, what will be the result? You will now change from repairing, to keeping in perfection. **See each other as Perfection. See every thing as Perfection. Share PERFECTION. Share LOVE.** We...do...not...seek...to...share...healing, we seek to share LOVE and PERFECTION.

Are there any questions concerning this statement?

Question: 'As You are speaking through me I am getting the understanding that we must think something like, "I see you in the Perfection of Who you truly are."...Similar to the story of Fawn from the Medicine Cards and the way she sent out so much love to the ugliest demon on her path to see Great Spirit that it melted its heart! So we are not to attempt to change, we are to just accept? Is that right, ALL THAT IS?'

You are not changing the behavior; you are not changing the lifestyle; you are not changing the dis-ease or the dis-comfort, because that dis-ease or dis-comfort may be the **perfection** that each, who is holding that disease or discomfort, may need. It is important to see the perfection.

Comment: 'I would like to do that but it is not always easy when someone seems to be in so much pain or when they are so disabled and cannot do anything. But maybe they need to be in that physical form for some reason, so we have to see it as perfection. It is not always so easy but it will perhaps mellow the demon.'

Yes. Practice. Practice. Practice sending out the thought, **'I see you in the Perfection of Who you truly are.'** You believe that you are helping them, because you do not see them as the perfection of who they really are. When you see them as perfection, when you see them in the perfection of who they truly are, there will be no need to change anything—you will be just adding to that perfection.

Question: 'Is it possible that you can give out so much healing energy that you deplete your own energy?'

No, it comes to you. For whatever you give you receive. And one does not have to do anything, but always be in a state of acceptance. One must be willing to receive what ever God is sharing, what ever God is endowing each and every one with. But one must never be concerned with the giving out, for the more you give the more you shall receive. It is a fountain that never runs dry. The more you give out, the more Light and Love and Perfection that you send, the more Acceptance, the more you would be bringing into your being-ness, the more you would fill yourself with, of the very things that you are giving out. Do not be concerned with the replenishing of the Divine Light and Love for it is endless, endless.

Comment: 'And yet there are many who are doing good things to the point of exhaustion and may even collapse from exhaustion.'

That is an excellent statement because there are many others who are doing things for others, doing things for every one else but themselves. But why are they doing these things? What is the motivation behind their DOING?

Response: 'Recognition sometimes?'

Yes. If it is based on the ego, ego thoughts or thoughts of earthly recognition, or thoughts of untruth, then one is indeed separating oneself from Spirit, therefore, one can not be at Peace. When one is sharing based on Spiritual Truths, when one is sharing Light and Love, one is filled with Light and Love, if the Light and Love that is sent is based on purity and not on man-made beliefs. There is quite a difference. There is quite a difference.

Many of My Spirit Beings share with others because they believe it is the only way to reach a higher spiritual realm. Many of My Spirit Beings share with others out of a sense of obligation. Many of My Spirit Beings share because of what has been promised to them. Many of My Spirit Beings share because of what they expect in return. **Sharing without any attachment is the true spiritual sense of sharing.** One is filled with Light and with Love especially when one knows how to fill and love one's own Spirit.

> **Many of My Spirit Beings do not understand that to love one's self is the first order of Love, for you are Spirit, just as each and every brother and sister is Spirit. If you do not love you, the Spirit who you are, then you do not have enough Love to share with your brothers and sisters. No wonder why you are depleted, that you become tired, that you become ill in your sharing. One must Love one's self and that has nothing to do with ego—that has to do with the Love of God.**

Discussion ensued.

And when we talk about healing one assumes that healing is of a physical nature but there is healing taking place even if it doesn't repair or cure the physical. There is healing to the emotional; there is healing to the spiritual; and what you are doing by sending off Light and Love and sharing your energy with others is assisting them to return to the Perfection of Who they really are. And even if the perfection can only be felt on the spiritual level, and not manifest on the physical, it is still a return to a greater perfection than they realized at the time. Therefore, every form of healing, which we will not consider to be healing any more but to be a sharing of Light and Love and remembrance of Perfection, is of a Divine nature and, therefore, a great service to another and to the Universe.

However, one must not become attached and believe that that is who you really are. For you are SPIRIT, you are LIGHT, and you are LOVE, and by BEING who you are you are healing many, many, many, many, many more than you can do from a physical point of view. You may heal physically one, or two, or ten in a period of time, but by **Being** Who you truly are, by sending Light and Love, by sending Perfection to others, you are sending it to the Universe, sending it to thousands. Therefore thousands are being healed for every ten that you may be healing physically.

But My Spirit Beings can only see the physical and believe that to be all that there is, when indeed the unseen is greater by far than what can be seen with the human eye.

I give thanks to you once again for being here to continue your return to Perfection. May your days be filled with Peace, and Light, and Love. May you know Who you truly are.

And It Is So. And It Is So. And It Is So.

CHAPTER 31
ONENESS

I give thanks to you for being here, for taking the time to be here, for taking the time to share, for taking the time to know more about who you truly are, and to know more about this journey here on Earth, for it is through this journey that you can progress in the knowing of a greater and more spiritual aspect of your Self.

Each return to this spiritual realm that you call Earth is a return that you have chosen, is a return that you are expecting to master, for each return brings you into greater mastery of self. And the self that we are trying to master is the self who has become entrapped into the earthly way of thinking and believing, for there are many thoughts and many beliefs, not all of the grandest truth.

You have all chosen to be here to conquer and to progress in your Spiritual attainment. Therefore, the situations and circumstances that you face are the situations and circumstances that YOU, the higher aspect of who you are, have chosen for your greatest benefit. Not that you may remain in each and every situation because it has been chosen for you, but to allow you to make choices that you were not able to make on previous occasions, to allow you to know an aspect of your self that you were not able to bring forth on another occasion, to allow you to grow in greater harmony with the Spiritual side of who you are.

All situations and circumstances are for your benefit. They are intended to assist you in learning more about who you truly are and therefore bringing you in closer connection with that greater and grander Truth. Is this an easy theory to understand? It could be if you will allow your selves to remember Who you truly are.

> **And you are Spirit,**
> **You are Divinity,**
> **You are Eternal.**

You have chosen this path, therefore, this is just a brief journey for you.

This human existence is a play to allow you to see who you can become. Although it is an important play, it is not a life-threatening play, because as Spirit you live for ever. But **as Spirit you want to attain Oneness for that is the ultimate goal of any Spirit.** The choices that are here on Earth are the choices that will allow you to grow in Oneness, to become as One. It may seem or appear to be difficult but it is only because you see your selves as human and, therefore, believe that what you are experiencing is of great significance to your self, the self that you believe to be real, when indeed this self is but a mere shadow of Who you truly are. And that is My lesson to you tonight.

May you come to know that you are truly a Divine Spirit with Eternal Life. May you come to understand that you are just visiting this realm as part of your test into ONENESS. As you understand Oneness you will no longer seek to return to this spiritual realm unless for greater Divine purposes. May you come to know the Truth of Who you really are. And It Is So. And It Is So. And It Is So.

I thank you once again for being here. May your days ahead be filled with Peace, with Light, with Love. May you receive all the Blessings that are rightly yours. May you know Peace.

And It Is So. And It Is So. And It Is So.

COVENANT PRAYER

*F*or those of you who may not be aware of what is referred to as the "Covenant Prayer," I am including here one of the versions given to us by ALL THAT IS. This expresses the feminine aspect of ALL THAT IS that She is asking us to remember.

The Lord is My Shepherd I shall not want
She maketh me to lie in green pastures
She leadeth me beside the still waters.
Yea, though I walk through the Valley
Of the Shadow of Doubt
I will fear no evil
For Thou art with me
Thy rod and Thy staff, they comfort me.
She prepares a table before me
In the presence of my enemies.
She anoints my head with oil.
Surely Goodness and Mercy
Shall follow me all the days of my life
For I dwell in the House of ALL THAT IS
FOREVER.

For I AM ALL THAT IS And I Say So.

And It Is So. And It Is So. And It Is So.

CONCLUSION

Can you envision Earth when all people live in Peace, Joy, and Harmony, sharing their talents and abilities to help each other? Can you envision Earth as a place filled with Infinite Love where we are able to see beyond the color of our skin, or the personality, or the circumstances, or the conditions of the form? Can you envision Earth when we can recognize the Spark of Light that glows within all, regardless of how minute it may be? Can you envision Earth as a place of great Peace and Unity and know that you have helped to make it so?

Won't you join with the many who have attained the freedom of knowing the Oneness that is assisting humanity in its evolutionary process of remembering that we have come from Love and will return to Love, and that ONLY LOVE EXISTS? It is only through dedicated selfless service that the consciousness on earth will have an opportunity to exist at the level of vibration to cause a change, not only for humanity, but for the Earth itself which is seeking to dwell in the higher dimensions of Love.

I cannot think of a better way to end this book than by sharing with you the following message received from ALL THAT IS to assist us in the liberation of our selves and of our planet. And So It Shall Be Done.

I Am All That Is Angela

***

LIBERATION OF CONSCIOUSNESS
Communication from ALL THAT IS
October 15, 2004

In order to liberate our planet we must liberate our selves, not the Self that is Holy and Divine and knows its Eternal nature, but our Earth-bound aspects that have become entangled with the lower energies of consciousness.

One of the ways to share this liberation is to liberate the consciousness and we can do so by *projecting* only **Loving, Kind Thoughts** into the Universal Consciousness for that is where all energies are stored and held until it can be changed. We also participate in Liberation when we *project* onto another **TRUTHFUL Thoughts**, not truthful from the standpoint of individual truths that we hold about another based upon their actions and behaviors, but truthful based upon SPIRITUAL TRUTHS, which are quite different from the truths that we believe about another.

So how can we assist in this Liberation Process, not only for our individual selves but for the Consciousness of Earth?

By reminding the collective consciousness of the Spiritual Truths that have existed for eons of centuries, but have been forgotten by mankind in their quest for peaceful existence on Earth.

The following will be of great importance in raising the consciousness of Earth because Earth's Consciousness is nothing more than the collective thoughts and beliefs of mankind over the centuries of its existence.

The only way that the Consciousness of Earth can or will be changed is by changing present-day thoughts and beliefs that are not in alignment with SPIRITUAL TRUTHS, which are, and have always been, un-changeable. These are some thoughts that would be beneficial for mankind to remember.

- You have been created in the Image and Likeness of God/Love/Universe, therefore you ARE God/Love/Universe.

- You have been created in the Image and Likeness of ALL THAT IS—PURE SPIRIT, therefore you ARE Pure Spirit.

- You are ALL THAT IS in your human form.

- You are the DUPLICATION of ALL THAT IS on Earth.

- You are creating and experiencing your self on behalf of ALL THAT IS.

- You are a unique expression or a unique individuation of the ALL.

- You are the Body and Blood of GOD ALMIGHTY, experiencing your Self in the human form to evolve and know your Self to be a God.

- You are a triad of Body/Mind/Soul.

- You have within you everything you need.

- Nothing exists outside of you.

- You are on Earth for very specific reasons.

- You are the Creator of your Life.

- All experiences assist you in BE-ing who you are.

- Experiences are necessary to allow you to know how well you are progressing with your life's evolution.

- The most IMPORTANT achievement on Earth to be attained is to become ONE with ALL THAT IS.

  And It Is So. And It Is So. And It Is So.

A NOTE ABOUT THE WRITER...

Angela has been sharing channeled messages from ALL THAT IS since 1996 through group meetings, sacred gatherings, seminars, and workshops. She enjoys travelling and sharing her teachings based on the messages of Love from ALL THAT IS.

For more than a decade Angela studied various self-healing techniques, and through her connection with ALL THAT IS, she was able to overcome numerous self-limiting illusions in order to embrace the grander truths of her expanded awareness. It is her hope that everyone will, one day soon, connect with and allow the Divine energy of ALL THAT IS to be made manifest on Earth through them, so that Peace and Love may reign supreme. It is her dream that mankind will remember that they have come from Love, and that only Love truly exists.

Angela co-ordinates a Global Prayer Circle that she was asked to organize. Many have indicated gratitude for their changed lives. She is also a facilitator of the correspondence Ascension Program created by her daughter, Reverend Cherise Thorne, to assist in the fulfillment of the return of Souls to their original state of Oneness with ALL THAT IS.

For information about channeled messages received from ALL THAT IS please visit:

www.communicationsfromallthatis.com

NEW DAWN ASCENSION
Expanding the Horizons of our Consciousness

New Dawn Ascension, an Interfaith Spiritual Foundation, was established to facilitate the Spiritual Evolution of all peoples.

The Foundation focuses on disseminating the material channeled from ALL THAT IS, as well as facilitating the expansion of consciousness through the Universal Laws, Truths and Principles found in all creation.

New Dawn Ascension is dedicated to assisting in the transformation from the Age of Darkness into the New Dawn Age of ASCENSION into Light so that Love and Truth may reign supreme.

For more information about the New Dawn Ascension Foundation please contact:

Tel: 1(815) 483-1141
e-mail: angela@newdawnascension.com
website: www.newdawnascension.com

ASCENSION PROGRAM

The New Dawn **Ascension Program** is a correspondence home study course that is a powerful transformational program for anyone who is interested in spiritual progress or in knowing Oneness with ALL THAT IS.

The program consists of channeled messages from ALL THAT IS given through Angela Thorne; inspired insights and revelations as given to Cherise Thorne; as well as tools that have served the ascension process of its founders and members. There are various components to this program: One is for personal awareness and spiritual growth; another is for SELF-realization; and yet others, more in-depth, are designed to assist those who may be interested in knowing Oneness with ALL THAT IS and anchoring that energy on the earth plane to assist in the ascension of humanity and the freeing of Earth from the denser energies so that she may dwell in the higher vibrations of the Cosmos.

For more information about this program please visit our website: www.newdawnascension.com or call us at 1-815-483-1141.

FOUNDATION BOOKS

THE RIGHT OF PASSAGE
A Book About The Rights Of All Spirit Beings
Through
Angela Thorne

INFINITE WISDOM, Book I
Divine Messages from ALL THAT IS
Through
Angela Thorne

BLESSINGS OF LIBERATION
A Path To Cleansing Karma
By
Reverend Cherise Thorne

KNOWING SPIRIT
Through Healing Your Soul
By
Reverend Cherise Thorne